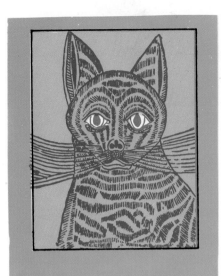

George and Lois Sage

THE
HISTORY
ATLAS OF
ASIA

The Macmillan Continental History Atlases

The History Atlas of Africa
The History Atlas of Asia
The History Atlas of Europe
The History Atlas of North America
The History Atlas of South America

THE

HISTORY

ATLAS OF

ASIA

Ian Barnes
and
Robert Hudson

Foreword by
Bhikhu Parekh

MACMILLAN • USA

MACMILLAN
A Simon & Schuster Macmillan Company
1633 Broadway
New York, NY 10019-6785

Library of Congress Cataloging-in-Publication Data

Barnes, Ian R., 1946–
  The Macmillan history atlas of Asia / Ian Barnes: foreword by
Bhikhu Parekh.
    p.   cm.
  Includes bibliographical references and index.
  ISBN 0–02–862581–1 (hardcover)
  1. Asia—Historical geography—Maps. I. Parekh, Bhikhu C.
II. Title. III. Title: History atlas of Asia. IV. Title: Atlas of
Asia.
 G2201.S1 B25 1998 <G&M>
 911'.5—DC21

                     97–52395
                       CIP
                     MAPS

Printed in the United States of America
10 9 8 7 6 5 4 3 2 1

FOREWORD

The History Atlas of Asia is a reliable and representative history covering nearly ten thousand years. Asia has seen the rise and fall of many civilizations, from Akkadia in Mesopotamia to the Mughal empire in India. This book is not narrowly political and gives attention to commerce, culture, philosophy, religion, and the economy. Accordingly, Roman links with India, the Silk Road, and the great Sri Vijayan commercial empire are studied and placed within the context of Asian geography, with its vast mountain ranges, desert, steppe, and jungle. The spread of religious ideas and philosophies—early Indo-European, Hinduism, Buddhism, Islam, Taoism, and Confucianism—are all treated as they migrated from one area to another with surprising ease, either by peaceful means or through violence. Changing borders and the forces shaping them are considered, as are the movement of peoples and invasions, such as the impact of the Tatars and the Ottoman Turks. The authors are fully aware that no single book can cover every aspect of Asian history, so they have exercised their professional judgment as wisely as possible in selecting what they consider to merit inclusion, with the aim of providing the reader with a more significant understanding of Asia. They demonstrate the process by which vastly different social and political structures have been developed by different Asian societies during broadly similar historical periods.

The historical facts are supported by carefully prepared maps that have a life of their own, as well as numerous illustrations. The atlas attempts to be highly imaginative and lucid and aims to excite readers to the additional study of more detailed histories. The reader's appetite is whetted further by frequent and fascinating asides, such as the role of veterinary services in Asokan India, drainage systems in Harappa, Persian art forms, T'ang poetry, and the spread of the Tatar cavalry.

The atlas demonstrates the importance of Asia as a "melting pot" of ideas, beliefs, and cultures that have provided the wider world with so much in terms of religion, medicine, literature, and knowledge. Now that Asia is regaining its rightful place in the world as an important political, economic, and cultural player on the world stage, no one can afford to remain ignorant of Asia's history and power. Through the process of globalization, the Asian economies are now highly linked and interwoven with Europe and the United States; this interdependence has become so great that financial crisis in Asia has an impact on the rest of the world. In the meantime China has developed into a strong military and economic power and deserves serious consideration.

This short book is intended to serve students as well as the interested lay reader as an introduction to the most populous continent in the world.

Bhikhu Parekh
University of Pennsylvania
South Asia Regional Studies

CONTENTS

THE

HISTORY

ATLAS OF

ASIA

PART I: ANCIENT CIVILIZATIONS

Between 8000 BC and 6000 BC, large communities arose in the four major river valleys of the Nile, the Tigris and Euphrates, the Indus, and the Huang Ho. Their growth and development was predicated upon the development of agriculture and the establishment of small settlements, which in turn developed into large urban communities. The key to the growth of urban settlements lay in the cultivation of cereal production made possible by extensive irrigation and the use of the flood plains adjacent to the river systems and deltas. Wheat and barley were grown extensively in Mesopotamia and India, while millet was cultivated in China.

During the ninth and eighth millennia BC large and permanent communities developed for the first time, employing brick and stone as building materials. The oldest and most developed of these cities was Jericho (Tell es-Sultan) in the Jordan Valley. Although largely an agricultural settlement in its origins, Jericho evolved into a major regional center.

An important development in agricultural techniques and production took place in the fifth millennium BC with the creation of effective irrigation systems allowing for the spread of settlement and the cultivation of once arid, semi-desert areas. As a result, many settlements appeared on the edges of the riverine plain of Mesopotamia. In China evidence of wet rice cultivation in the region of the lower Yangtze exists from about 5000 BC, due to improved methods of irrigation.

The importance of irrigation systems and of river systems cannot be overemphasized, since the control of river systems meant not only richer agricultural yields and growth, but also

Neolithic "Tahunian" javelin and arrowheads from Jericho, c. 6500–5500 BC.

domination over rival communities. For example, one of the major economic and strategic issues that arose in Mesopotamia in the second millennium was the control of the waters of the Euphrates and Tigris Rivers, and the struggle over water rights that ensued, which led to conflict between neighboring city-states. Some methods would include damming the water above rival cities, to deprive them of water for irrigation, eventually to be followed by the sudden release of the dam to create widespread flooding, as happened in Larsa c. 1750 under the Babylonian king Hammurabi.

Similarly, the impact of nature upon river systems could have devastating effects upon societies, as when complex shifts in the river course of the Indus River left fields destroyed, disrupted trade, and ultimately resulted in the end of the Indus civilization after 2000 BC. By way of comparison, archaeological excavations have shown that between c. 1766 and 1122 BC, under the Shang in China, the capital of the Chinese state moved several times due to the flooding of the Yellow River.

Once the ancient communities had moved away from subsistence farming, by the fourth millennium in Mesopotamia, more individuals could engage in other specializations, such as metalwork and building, along with other crafts, such as pottery, ceramics, and jewelry. Harnessed to and stimulated by a growth in commerce and transit trade between the communities of Mesopotamia, Asia Minor, and Greece, came the rise of true civilizations built upon the development of city-states. In turn these city-states traded among themselves, with overland routes from the Indus Valley to Persia and Afghanistan, which allowed the transport of gold, silver, copper, turquoise, and lapis lazuli.

Among the great civilizations in Asia that arose were the Sumerians in Mesopotamia (c. 3000 BC), the civilization of the Indus Valley (after c. 2700 BC), and the civilization of Shang China (before c. 1500 BC), although signs of the development of more sophistication in culture and society in China can be dated from about 2500 BC.

As the cities developed as true state societies in the Near East by the third millennium, they became administrative and manufacturing centers of urban civilization administered by a ruler and literate elites. The city-states differed greatly from the earlier cities such as Jericho, which had simply served as agglomerations of population, since they demanded administration and organization and a high degree of social and economic organization. This necessitated the development of written languages, which allowed for greater sophistication in communication and a degree of centralized control in the hands of a ruling elite, who controlled the bureaucracies for the administrative functioning of societies and the armies for external security.

Increased literacy was crucial to the early civilizations, for the development of law codes, tax records, and accounts, which have also provided historians with their knowledge of these ancient societies. For example, Hittite royal archives in the second millennium BC contained a wealth of historical information concerning government, religion, and mythology in the Hittite society.

In Mesopotamia and adjacent regions, cuneiform script was first employed by the Sumerians, then by the Akkadians, Babylonians, Assyrians, and Hittites. The influence of Sumeria had proved to be so great that it had lasted long after the demise of the Sumerians.

Archaeological excavations in Ur, Kish, Eridu, and other cities have unearthed clay tablets with cuneiform inscriptions that recorded commercial transactions, and in a later period bore works of a religious, literary, and scientific nature. Historians have been provided with a wealth of material on Babylonian and Sumerian societies such as the Epic of Gilgamesh, which tells us much about the belief systems of Sumerian society in its account of the fruitless search for immortality by Gilgamesh, the Great King of Uruk, as well as emphasizing man's dependence upon the forces of nature, and most notably the hazards of flooding. Similarly, we have learned about the regulation and legislation of society from the discovery of Hammurabi's law code, dating from the second millennium, which was recorded on a stele in the cuneiform script of Akkadian, the successor to the Sumerian language.

In China the use of pictograms was discovered in the excavation of Shang sites at An-yang. Not only have historians been able to learn more about Shang society in the second millennium, but also these discoveries have demonstrated the early use of the longest-used script in the world, which has ensured the

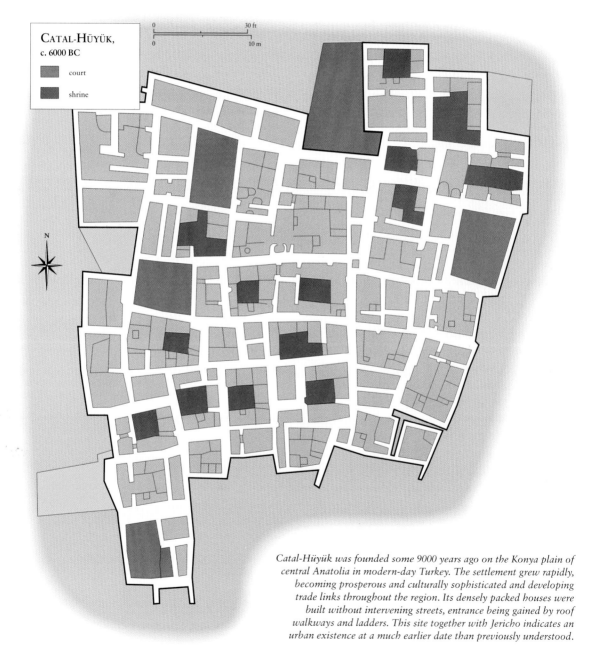

CATAL-HÜYÜK,
c. 6000 BC

court

shrine

Catal-Hüyük was founded some 9000 years ago on the Konya plain of central Anatolia in modern-day Turkey. The settlement grew rapidly, becoming prosperous and culturally sophisticated and developing trade links throughout the region. Its densely packed houses were built without intervening streets, entrance being gained by roof walkways and ladders. This site together with Jericho indicates an urban existence at a much earlier date than previously understood.

continuity of Chinese civilization, despite long periods of turmoil and political change.

Similarly, the Indus Valley witnessed the arrival of the Indo-Europeans, who overran the Harappan civilization and spread their faith in the god Indra not only through the sword but also through their Vedic texts. This was at the beginning of the second millennium BC, and their language, Sanskrit, became the vehicle for spreading the oldest known sacred texts. Classical Sanskrit, written in the Devanagari alphabet, would be used as the standard language of Hindu scholarship and literature between c. 500 BC and AD 1000. Much later, it was discovered that there was a similarity of Sanskrit to Latin and Greek, and this discovery became a major contribution to the development of comparative philology during the European Enlightenment in the late eighteenth century.

One of the greatest advances in the development of urban civilizations was that of metallurgy and technology. Metallurgy has been an important indicator of the ancient civilizations, since metals became an increasingly important material. For example, with copper abundant in the highlands of the Near East, copper metallurgy developed in Mesopotamia in the fourth and third millennia BC. This led to a knowledge of the working of other materials and the use of metals to produce tools and weapons and for decorative purposes. Finds in China have shown that bronze casting had been fully developed by the Shang, c. 1766–1122 BC, with inscribed bronze artifacts demonstrating the existence of a written language from c. 1500 BC.

In Mesopotamia, in the fourth and third millennia, organized religions played an important role in society, both in spreading belief systems and in the carrying out of administration from the temples. Such activities probably included regulated food distribution in times of poor harvests. The ziggurats in the temple of Uruk symbolized a transcendental link between heaven and earth in a society that believed that kings came from heaven and that laws were granted by the gods, who in their anthropomorphic forms provided for the security of the people and the fertility of the crops and livestock. The deities were responsible for different needs. Among them could be found Anu, the god of heaven; Enki, the god of water; and Enlil, the god of the earth.

In some societies kings would act as supreme high priests, as in the Hittite empire in the second millennium BC. By comparison, in Shang China the nobility officiated in the rites of ancestor worship and of a wide variety of fertility and nature cults. This might also explain the absence of a separate priestly caste, before the arrival in the fifth century of Taoism, a philosophy that advocated complete withdrawal from worldly affairs and submission to contemplative calm, spread through China by its founder, Lao-tze.

Some societies demonstrated great tolerance to other divinities, such as the Hittites, who tolerated Anatolian, Hurrian, and Syrian gods, or much later, during the sixth century BC, under the Persian rulers Cyrus and Darius, who tolerated the beliefs, practices, and institutions of all the constituent subject peoples under their rule, thus unifying their peoples into a great and powerful empire.

EARLIEST SETTLEMENTS, C. 8000 BC

In 8000 BC, the world was peopled by small bands of hunter-gatherers. Within two thousand years, substantial villages and small towns developed in four major river valleys—the Nile, Tigris and Euphrates, the Indus, and the Huang Ho. This phenomenom was occasioned by the parallel birth of agriculture. The cultivation of cereals made possible the growth of larger communities; irrigation and the use of flood plains allowed the extensive use of wheat and barley in Mesopotamia and India, and millet in China. With the end of subsistence farming, fewer people were needed to farm, so some could pursue other roles, thus leading to craft specialization and socially differentiated societies. Early settlements acquired skills in metalwork, brickmaking, architecture, jewelry, sculpture, and town building. Trade networks evolved, and the Indus Valley became linked with Mesopotamia, Asia Minor, and Greece. The societies springing up in these areas created states, built cities, and developed writing. The increased sophistication of society required a measure of centralized control, a secular ruler or priestly elite, bureaucracies, and armies for defense. The administration of city-states and kingdoms was aided by literacy. Accounts, records, and laws required a knowledge of writing. In Mesopotamia and surrounding areas, a wedge-shaped cuneiform script was adopted by Sumerians, Akkadians, Babylonians, Assyrians, and Hittites. Pictographs spread to the Indus Valley; Chinese pictograms inscribed on animal shoulder blades have been found in the excavation of Shang sites at An-yang.

The growth of wealthy cities required fortifications, new weaponry, and large armies, as rivalry between states led to larger and larger kingdoms as smaller and weaker states were conquered. Much is known about Sumer and its ziggurat of Ur, and of Sargon the Akkadian. Babylon was mentioned by the biblical prophet Isaiah as the "glory of kingdoms." Catal-Hüyük, on the Turkish Konya plateau, was built of houses tightly packed for defense; this town of some 6,000 people existed c. 6000 BC. They grew barley, wheat, and lentils, used obsidian tools and mirrors, traded for Syrian flint, wove high-quality woollen textiles, worshiped animal gods, painted murals, and made jewelry from shells. In China, a Neolithic Yang-shao culture flourished (c. 3950–1700 BC) in Shensi and Shansi. The farmers used slash and burn methods of agriculture, grew millet, and raised pigs, supplementing this diet with the products of hunting and fishing. The succeeding Lung-Shan culture (c. 2000–1850 BC) was more developed than Yang-shao, with permanent villages owning herds and flocks of cattle, sheep, goats, and pigs. The feudal Shang dynasty (c. 1500–1000 BC) arose in An-yang. Royal tombs contain bronze and jade objects, musical instruments, and pottery. War was common, and Shang pictograms show soldiers with dagger-axes, an early form of halberd.

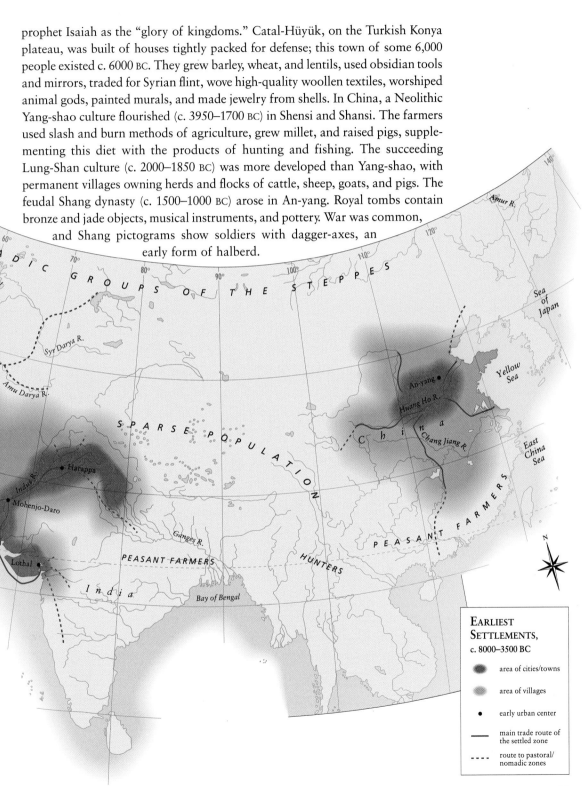

EARLIEST SETTLEMENTS,
c. 8000–3500 BC

⬤ area of cities/towns

⬤ area of villages

• early urban center

— main trade route of the settled zone

--- route to pastoral/nomadic zones

MESOPOTAMIA, C. 2279 BC

> "Gilgamesh replied: 'Where is the Man who can clamber to heaven? Only the gods live for ever with glorious Shamash, but as for us men, our days are numbered, our occupations are a breath in the wind.'"
> *The Epic of Gilgamesh*

This tumbler, made in Susa around 3500 BC, typifies the brilliant painted pottery produced by skilled Iranians. Its design is based on an ibex with vastly exaggerated horns.

Lying in western Asia, Mesopotamia was one of the cradles of human civilization. A flat and hot landscape made up of marshes and plains, Mesopotamia stretched from Nineveh in the north to the Persian Gulf in the south, and between the rivers Tigris in the west and the Euphrates, spreading farther east to the Zagros Mountains.

With an agricultural economy, reliant upon widespread development of irrigation systems across its fertile plains, Mesopotamia, under the Sumerians, witnessed the earliest development of cities in the fourth millennium BC, with estimated populations of 10,000 inhabitants or more. These cities grew into city-states, stimulated by a growth in commerce and transit trade. Nevertheless, the region was subject to destructive floods from the Tigris and other Mesopotamian rivers, which had made the development of irrigation systems so crucial.

The lack of local timber, rocks, and metals meant that urban architecture was constructed of sun-dried clay. Of particular note are the magnificently decorated temples with their ziggurats, such as at the temple of Uruk. These buildings symbolized the transcendental link between heaven and earth in a society that believed that kings came from heaven and that laws were granted by the gods, who, in their anthropomorphic forms, provided for the security of the people and the fertility of the crops and livestock. The deities were responsible for different needs. Among them could be found Anu, the god of heaven; Enki, the water god; and Enlil, the god of earth.

The temples, with their priests, scholars, teachers, mathematicians, and astrologers, served as academic centers of excellence and also acted as food distribution centers in times of crisis.

Hand in hand with the rise of the city came the invention of writing among the Sumerians of southern Mesopotamia. Archaeological excavations in Ur, Kish, Eridu, and other cities have unearthed clay tablets with cuneiform inscriptions that record commercial transactions, and in a later period bear works of a religious, literary, and scientific nature. Most notable of these works is the Epic of Gilgamesh, found on clay tablets in Uruk recounting the fruitless search for

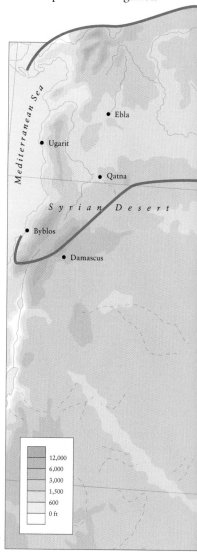

Mediterranean Sea

- Ebla
- Ugarit
- Qatna

Syrian Desert

- Byblos
- Damascus

| 12,000 |
| 6,000 |
| 3,000 |
| 1,500 |
| 600 |
| 0 ft |

immortality of Gilgamesh, the Great King of Uruk.

So great was the influence of the Sumerian language that it lasted long after the Sumerian demise, following the conquest of Mesopotamia in the third millennium BC by the Akkadians, a Semitic people from the Zagros Mountains, Arabia, and Persia. The Akkadians, tempted by the spoils of the great Sumerian city-states, were united by Sargon (c. 2334–2279 BC), who developed trade routes to the northeast and to Asia Minor in the west. We know little of the Akkadian dynasty, nor even of the precise whereabouts of Sargon's capital at Agade.

Eventually the Akkadians fell to the Gutians, who invaded from the Zagros Mountains, to be succeeded in turn by a Sumerian dynasty, which established a well-organized and highly developed empire in the last century of the third millennium BC.

Cast in bronze, this almost life-sized bust of Sargon dates from around 2270 BC.

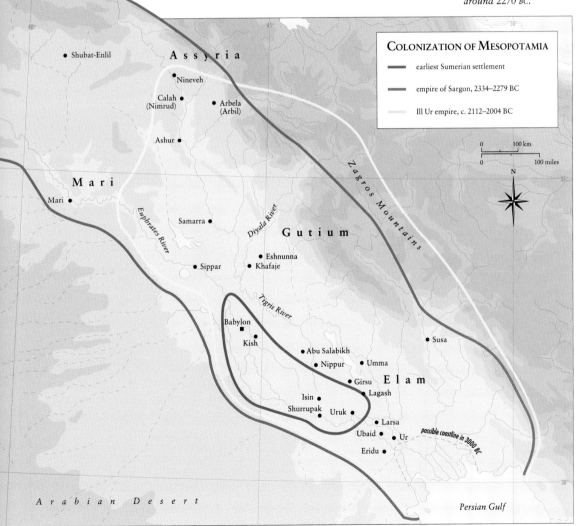

COLONIZATION OF MESOPOTAMIA

- earliest Sumerian settlement
- empire of Sargon, 2334–2279 BC
- Ill Ur empire, c. 2112–2004 BC

Shubat-Enlil

Assyria

Nineveh
Calah (Nimrud)
Arbela (Arbil)
Ashur

Mari

Mari
Samarra
Euphrates River
Diyala River

Gutium

Zagros Mountains

Eshnunna
Khafaje
Sippar

Tigris River

Babylon
Kish
Abu Salabikh
Nippur
Umma
Girsu
Elam
Lagash
Isin
Shurrupak
Uruk
Larsa
Ubaid
Ur
Eridu
Susa

possible coastline in 3000 BC

Arabian Desert

Persian Gulf

0   100 km
0   100 miles
N

CIVILIZATION OF THE INDUS VALLEY, c. 2750 BC

The fertile alluvial land around the Indus River and its tributaries was home to the earliest known civilization of South Asia. It covered some 500,000 square miles, extending from the Arabian Sea, the Rann of Cutch, and the Gulf of Cambay through the Punjab, Sind, and Uttar Pradesh to southern Afghanistan. Lasting about 1,000 years, this sophisticated culture paralleled Bronze Age Egypt, Mesopotamia, and Crete. Roughly one hundred settlements are known, many being large towns, with the largest at Harappa and Mohenjo-Daro, each having a three-mile circumference. The former supplies the term Harappan to the entire Indus culture. Excavations have revealed uniform grid patterns of streets, with solid mud-brick buildings and elaborate drainage systems, surrounded by defensive walls and overlooked by a citadel.

The housing comprises two types. Larger homes at Mohenjo-Daro consist of a number of rooms grouped around a courtyard with stairs leading to an upper story or flat roof; poorer people lived in single-room huts. Some houses had bathrooms with toilets linked to street drains. Mohenjo-Daro was an important trading and manufacturing center possessing workshops for potters, known for terra-cotta figures, dyers, metalworkers, and beadworkers. This flourishing maritime trade, using Bahrain (Dilmun) as a way station, was accompanied by overland routes from the Indus Valley to Afghanistan for gold, silver, copper, and lapis lazuli, and Persia for turquoise. A possible Harappan trading center was established at Shorthugai, over 600 miles to the north of Harappa, facilitating long-distance trade. Goods were transported by bullock carts and riverine and maritime vessels, as characterized in models and carvings on seals. Harappan civilization was founded on the Indus, which floods each year, very like the Nile. The annual deposits of fertile silt allowed the planting of wheat and barley, while rice was grown at some settlements; peas, mustard, and dates were other dietary elements. Fragments of woven cotton cloth from Mohenjo-Daro demonstrate the cultivation of cotton and are the earliest evidence of cotton textiles in Asia. The inhabitants kept a variety of domestic animals such as cattle, sheep, goats, fowl, boar, and elephants. Hunting of deer and wild boar probably took place in dense forest along the rivers. Knowledge of social, political, and religious organization in the Indus civilization is very limited. However, the development from pre-Harappan urban life to a complex culture uniting many cities with a uniform system of weights, brick sizes, and script (probably Dravidian) suggests a powerful central authority. The absence of palaces and statues representing rulers might indicate that governing elites were a merchant class or priests; some seals appear to depict a prototype Siva.

The Indus civilization came to an end after 2000 BC when complex shifts in the river course left fields destroyed and trade disrupted, forcing the abandonment of settlements and society's return to agricultural villages. Another factor explaining Harappan decline was the arrival of the Indo-Europeans, who rapidly conquered the area, as evidenced in earlier Vedic texts describing the god Indra as destroying walled cities and forts.

Indus figurines were often crudely made, like this clay "Mother-goddess," formed without any real attempt at precise modelling.

Sutkagen-Dór

Sotka-Koh

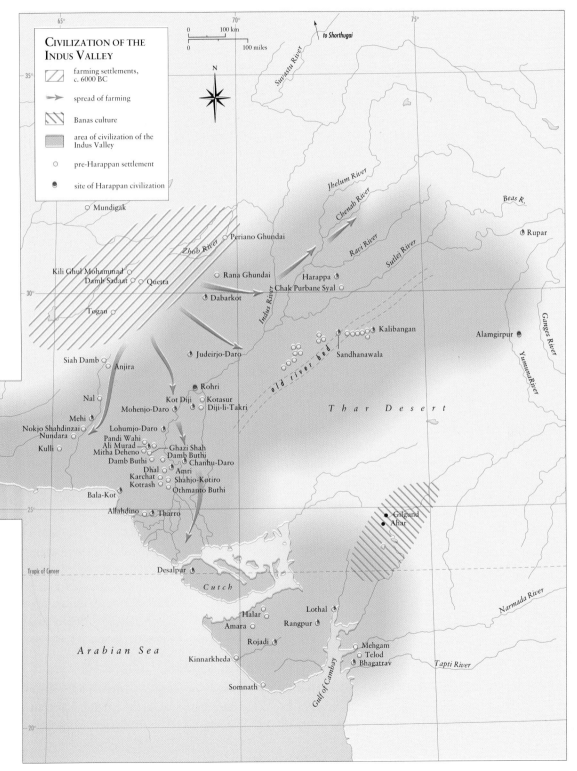

CIVILIZATION OF THE INDUS VALLEY

- ▨ farming settlements, c. 6000 BC
- → spread of farming
- ▧ Banas culture
- ▦ area of civilization of the Indus Valley
- ○ pre-Harappan settlement
- ◐ site of Harappan civilization

N

to Shorthugai

Swastu River

Jhelum River

Chenab River

Beas R.

Ravi River

Sutlej River

○ Mundigak

Zhob River

○ Periano Ghundai

Kili Ghul Mohammad ○
Damb Sadaat ○ ○ Quetta

○ Rana Ghundai

Harappa ◐

Chak Purbane Syal ○

◉ Rupar

○ Togau

Indus River

◐ Dabarkot

Ganges River

○ Siah Damb
○ Anjira

◐ Judeirjo-Daro

Kalibangan
Sandhanawala

◉ Alamgirpur

Yamuna River

○ Nal

◐ Rohri

Kot Diji ○ ○ Kotasur
Mohenjo-Daro ◐ ○ Diji-li-Takri

old river bed

T h a r   D e s e r t

Mehi ◐

Nokjo Shahdinzai ○
Nundara ○

Lohumjo-Daro ○

Kulli ○

Pandi Wahi ○
Ali Murad ○ — Ghazi Shah
Mitha Deheno ○ Damb Buthi ○
Damb Buthi ○ ◐ Chanhu-Daro
Dhal ○ Amri ◐
Karchat ○ Shahjo-Kotiro ○
Kotrash ○ Othmanto Buthi ○

Bala-Kot ○

Allahdino ○ ◐ Tharro

● Gilgund
● Ahar

Tropic of Cancer

Desalpur ◐

C u t c h

Narmada River

A r a b i a n   S e a

Halar ○
Amara ○ Rangpur ◐

Lothal ◐

Rojadi ◐

Kinnarkheda ○

Mehgam ◐
Telod ○
Bhagatrav ◐

Gulf of Cambay

Tapti River

Somnath ○

THE BABYLONIAN EMPIRE

Centered on the city of Babylon in southern Mesopotamia, the Babylonian state grew from a small kingdom in 1894 BC during the reign of the Amorite King Sumuabum into an empire that would eventually unify the whole of Mesopotamia.

The most noted ruler of the Amorite dynasty was Hammurabi (c. 1792–1750 BC), whose reign witnessed a flowering of cultural and intellectual achievements, including the first code of laws in history, which have been recorded upon a stele in the cuneiform script of Akkadian, successor to the Sumerian language.

Many Babylonian boundary marker stones, or "divine" markers, were erected to remind travelers, both spiritual and human, whose territory they were about to enter.

Hammurabi conquered the surrounding city-states of southern Mesopotamia, establishing an empire that extended into parts of Assyria (northern Iraq) while maintaining its heartland around Babylon and Kish. Once Hammurabi had brought Mesopotamia under single rule, the supremacy of Babylon would last for two centuries.

One of the key economic and strategic issues of the day was the control of the waters of the Euphrates River, and a struggle over water rights; not only did this involve the building of canals and irrigation systems for agriculture, but it also led to a conflict between neighboring city-states. Hammurabi's main rival was Rim-Sin, king of Larsa, a city-state situated downstream from Babylon. Hammurabi conquered Uruk and Isin in 1787 BC and then turned his attentions in a northerly and easterly direction. Over the next twenty years, there followed a series of coalitions between the Kingdoms of Mari, Ashur, Eshnunna, Babylon, and Larsa, followed by almost continuous warfare between 1764 BC and the time of Hammurabi's death in 1750 BC. During this time, Hammurabi found himself at war with a coalition made up of Ashur, Eshnunna, and Elam, the main powers of the Tigris, who were blocking off Babylon's access to metals from Iran. Hammurabi responded by damming the waters above Larsa, depriving Rim-Sin of water, then suddenly releasing the dam to create widespread flooding and destruction.

Nevertheless, the commercial wealth and political and cultural prestige of Babylon made the empire particularly attractive to foreign invasion. Gradually Babylonian culture waned under continued invasions from the Hittites, who sacked the capital in 1595 BC, thus bringing the First Dynasty of Babylon to an end. Babylon was then invaded by the Kassites, the Hurrians, and the Mittani.

By the end of the fifteenth century BC, the Assyrians, originating from the city of Ashur in northern Mesopotamia, rose in prominence, and had established an empire by the mid-fourteenth century that had conquered large areas from the Mittani, the Kassites, and the Hittites, ultimately affording the Assyrians control of much of former Babylonia.

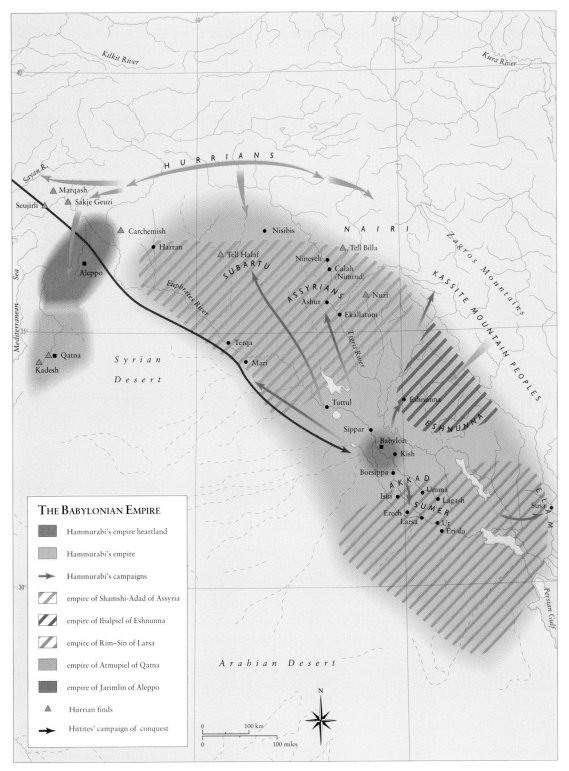

THE BABYLONIAN EMPIRE

- Hammurabi's empire heartland
- Hammurabi's empire
- → Hammurabi's campaigns
- empire of Shamshi-Adad of Assyria
- empire of Ibalpiel of Eshnunna
- empire of Rim–Sin of Larsa
- empire of Atmupiel of Qatna
- empire of Jarimlin of Aleppo
- ▲ Hurrian finds
- → Hittites' campaign of conquest

THE HITTITE EMPIRE

The Hittites, an ancient Indo-European people probably originating beyond the Black Sea, invaded Anatolia in the second millennium BC. After battles with the native population, the Hittites, under Labarna, conquered nearly all central Anatolia and founded their capital at Hattusas (present-day Bogazkoy). Early kings such as Hattusilis (1650–1620 BC) extended control over much of Anatolia and parts of northern Syria, and his grandson, Mursilis, defeated Aleppo and conquered Babylon (c. 1590 BC). The assassination of Mursilis inaugurated a period of internal strife and weakness finally ended by Telepinus (1530 BC). His Edict of Telepinus issued firm laws governing royal succession to end lawlessness, and designated the nobility as a high court to try constitutional crimes. The most powerful Hittite king was Suppilulinmas I (1380–1346 BC). His greatest enemy was the Mittani kingdom, which was soon destroyed, with Ugarit, Aleppo, and Carchemish becoming Hittite dependencies. The Assyrians, ruled by the Mittani, shook off their overlords and established their own state based on the capital at Ashur, but a Mittani rump state survived as a buffer between the two rival empires. Through constant hostilities, Hittite power percolated toward the Aegean Sea, into Armenia, and southward into Lebanon. Conflict with Egypt now seemed likely, and in the struggle for Syria and Lebanon, the Hittite king Mutuwallis fought Pharaoh Ramases II at Kadesh. Ramases claimed victory, but the Hittites retained Syria; the situation was regulated by treaty in 1275 BC concluding a mutual defense agreement and a dynastic marriage. Soon after 1200 BC, the Hittite kingdom collapsed under attack from the migrating Sea Peoples, and central Anatolia was swamped by Phrygians. Nevertheless, some city-states emerged retaining a Hittite identity, the most famous being Carchemish. Elsewhere, Hattusas was burned, like many Anatolian cities, as was Ugarit in Syria. The Hittites, as with Bronze Age civilizations in Mycenaen Greece and Crete, were swept away in a deluge of fire, which was eventually stopped by a powerful Egypt.

In this sculpture from the King's Gate of the capital, Hattusas, a Hittite warrior, is represented in the form of a deity.

Our knowledge of the Hittites derives from Egyptian records and from Hittite royal archives discovered at Hattusas. The texts are written using a cuneiform system and also hieroglyphs, and contain historical information and stories. Apparently, the king acted as supreme priest, military commander, and chief judge. After his death, he was deified. The nobility were advisors to the king, but they were eventually displaced by a bureaucracy. The empire was ruled through provincial governors, and some territories on the borders of the empire were vassal kingdoms. Unusual features of Hittite life were that war was conducted in a relatively humane fashion and the administration of justice was lenient, seldom imposing the death sentence or corporal punishment. Justice rested on the notion of restitution by restoring stolen property or financial recompense. In religious affairs, the king was the earthly representative of the storm god or weather god, which coexisted with a sun goddess, these being the main Hittite deities. Although knowledge of religious customs is incomplete, the Hittites seemed to be tolerant of other Anatolian divinities as well as Hurrian and Syrian gods.

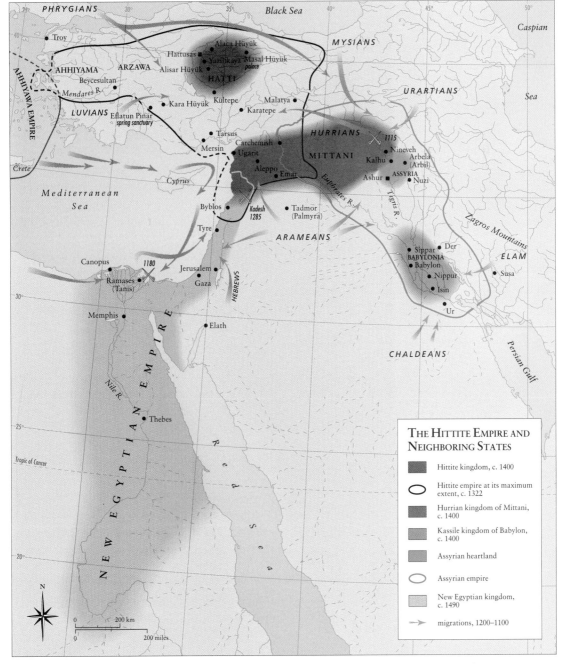

THE HITTITE EMPIRE AND NEIGHBORING STATES

- Hittite kingdom, c. 1400
- Hittite empire at its maximum extent, c. 1322
- Hurrian kingdom of Mittani, c. 1400
- Kassile kingdom of Babylon, c. 1400
- Assyrian heartland
- Assyrian empire
- New Egyptian kingdom, c. 1490
- migrations, 1200–1100

BRONZE AGE CHINA

Civilization developed in China at a later date than in Mesopotamia, Egypt, and India. Farming developed around 5800 BC, millet along the Yellow River basin, and rice along the wetlands of the east coast and Yangtze Valley, where the Yang-shao, 5000–3200 BC, and later the Long-shan cultures, 3200–1800 BC, emerged. Traditionally, the expansion of Chinese civilization, and the cultural influence and protofeudalism of the Shang dynasty, have been dated between c. 1766 and 1122 BC. The Shang state was centered on the valley of the Huang Ho River, which flowed through present-day Honan, Shantung, and Shensi Provinces into the Yellow Sea. Several communities were ruled by the strongest city-state, the Shang, whose capital moved several times, due, no doubt, to the flooding of the Yellow River. Armed with bronze weapons and chariots, the Shang nobility, a warrior caste, carried out military operations into the south, thus spreading Shang culture and political hegemony.

Later, between the eighth and third centuries of the first millennium BC, protofeudalism developed into true feudalism, with rule carried out by a tribal nobility who owed allegiance to the king based upon land in exchange for military service. This was during the period of the Chou dynasty, a people formerly subject to the Shang, who replaced them following the revolt of Wu Wang against Chou-hsin in c. 1122 BC. In reality the "son of heaven" now held little power over his nobility, in a period that has since been called the Time of the Warring States (403 to 221 BC). In turn the peasantry were tied to the land, which was, archaeologists have shown, already the world's most populous region by the seventh century BC.

The Shang used bronze ritual cauldrons in ancestor worship. These were sometimes decorated with primitive faces, a reference to an earlier period of human sacrifice.

Archaeological finds have also demonstrated that the art of bronze casting had already been fully mastered by the Shang and that inscribed bronze artifacts and oracle bones bear witness to the existence of a written language from c. 1500 BC. The use of the longest-used script in the world by the Chinese has ensured the continuity of Chinese civilization, despite the sporadic occurrence of rebellions, upheavals, and the anarchy of warlordism throughout Chinese history. Furthermore, the literate nobility were now no longer just a warrior caste, but had also become responsible for carrying out governmental duties in the beginnings of a bureaucratic system that was formed under the Chou. That the nobility also officiated in the rites of ancestor worship and a wide variety of fertility and nature cults might also explain why there was an absence of a separate priestly caste. From the fifth century, Taoism, a philosophy that advocated complete withdrawal from worldly affairs and submission to contemplative calm, was spread throughout China by its founder, Lao-tze, and his followers.

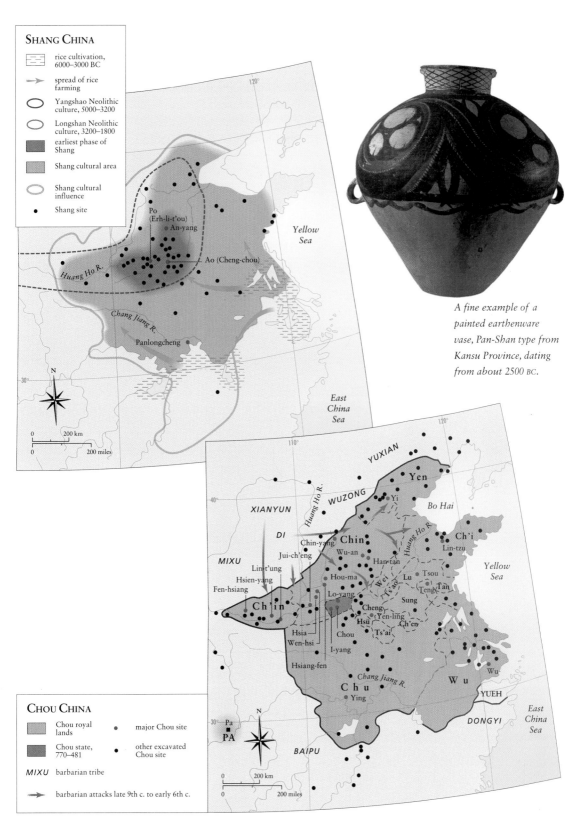

SHANG CHINA

- ▱ rice cultivation, 6000–3000 BC
- → spread of rice farming
- ⬭ Yangshao Neolithic culture, 5000–3200
- ⬭ Longshan Neolithic culture, 3200–1800
- ▪ earliest phase of Shang
- ▪ Shang cultural area
- ⬭ Shang cultural influence
- • Shang site

Po (Erh-li-t'ou)
An-yang
Ao (Cheng-chou)

Yellow Sea

Huang Ho R.

Chang Jiang R.

Panlongcheng

N

0   200 km
0   200 miles

East China Sea

A fine example of a painted earthenware vase, Pan-Shan type from Kansu Province, dating from about 2500 BC.

YUXIAN

XIANYUN

WUZONG

Yen

DI

Chin-yang
Wu-an

Chin

Yi

Bo Hai

Ch'i
Lin-tzu

MIXU

Jui-ch'eng

Han-tan

Yellow Sea

Lin-t'ung

Hou-ma

Wei

Lu
Tsou

Hsien-yang

Lo-yang

Ts'ao

Teng
Tan

Fen-hsiang

Ch'in

Cheng
Hsü

Sung

Yen-ling
Ch'en

Hsia
Wen-hsi

Chou
I-yang

Ts'ai

Hsiang-fen

Chang Jiang R.

Wu
Wu

Chu

YUEH

Ying

Pa

DONGYI

East China Sea

PA

N

BAIPU

0   200 km
0   200 miles

CHOU CHINA

- ▪ Chou royal lands
- ▪ Chou state, 770–481
- *MIXU* barbarian tribe
- → barbarian attacks late 9th c. to early 6th c.
- • major Chou site
- • other excavated Chou site

25

THE INDO-EUROPEANS

During the second millennium BC, the Indus Valley civilization declined and had nearly disintegrated when the Aryans, descendants of Indo-Europeans, migrated into India from the Hindu Kush. The significance of these peoples lies in not only their language but also their political and social impact on India. The existence of an extensive Sanskrit and ancient Greek literature, together with the more recently deciphered Hittite, shows characteristics of a common root language, called Proto-Indo-European. By 2000 BC, the ancient literatures were the product of distinct languages, suggesting that their original language was fairly unified about a thousand years earlier. Thereafter, Proto-Indo-European evolved into subfamilies such as Albanian, Armenian, Baltic, Celtic, Italic (Romance languages), Slavic, and Tocharian (spoken in medieval Chinese Turkestan). Comparative linguistics have shown how languages have developed, changed meanings, lost inflections, and moved toward modern forms. However, some common words provide interesting evidence of a unified heritage (father—English; Vater—German; pater—Latin; athir—Old Irish; pacer—Tocharian). The Indo-Iranian subfamily includes the Indic branch made up of ancient Sanskrit; the medieval Prakrit languages; and modern tongues such as Hindi, Urdu, Marathi, Bengali, and Gujerati.

An image of Agni, the Vedic god of fire and the hearth. In Sanskrit, the name Agni is linked linguistically with the Latin word ignis *(fire) and the English word* ignition.

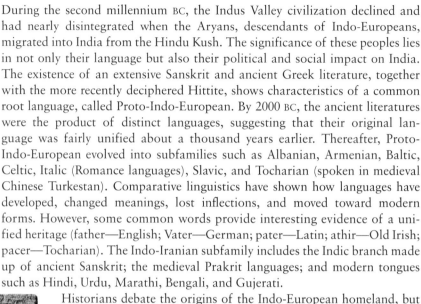

Historians debate the origins of the Indo-European homeland, but archaeological discoveries in the 1960s of a specific grave style of a prehistoric Kurgan culture suggest a strong likelihood that Indo-Europeans were a nomadic group roaming, between 5000 and 3000 BC, the steppes west of the Ural Mountains. They moved then into eastern Europe and northern Iran, from where they invaded India. The Aryan invasion and settlement of northern India is attested by the oldest literary document of India, the Rig Veda. The hymns of the Rig Veda fail to contain any mention of the Aryan migration but have many references to the battles that took place against the pre-Aryan inhabitants of the Indus civilization. They were known as *dasa,* the word coming to mean "slaves." They were held to be inferior because of their darker color and less angular features. They were demonized "untouchable," signifying an origin of the eventual caste system. The battles also destroyed cities, the Indus civilization. A Vedic hymn to Agni, the fire god, provides good evidence: "Through fear of you the dark people went away, not giving battle, leaving behind their possessions, when O Vaisvanara burning brightly for Puru, and destroying cities, you did shine." The Aryans introduced a retrograde culture into India, since the Harappan civilization was superior to the preurban, seminomadic, cattle-rearing Aryans. Cattle raids and intertribal fighting were common but did not prevent Aryan chariots spearheading the conquest of the Punjab, the Delhi region, and the Ganges Valley. They settled down to farming, redeveloped trade, and created kingdoms. The importance of the Aryans lies in their contribution of forest clearance for extensive agriculture, the idea of caste and religious sacrifice, the Sanskrit language, and the philosophy of the Upanishads.

DEVELOPMENT OF THE INDO-EUROPEAN LANGUAGES
(After Tomas Gamkrelidze and Vyacheslav Ivanov, 1985)

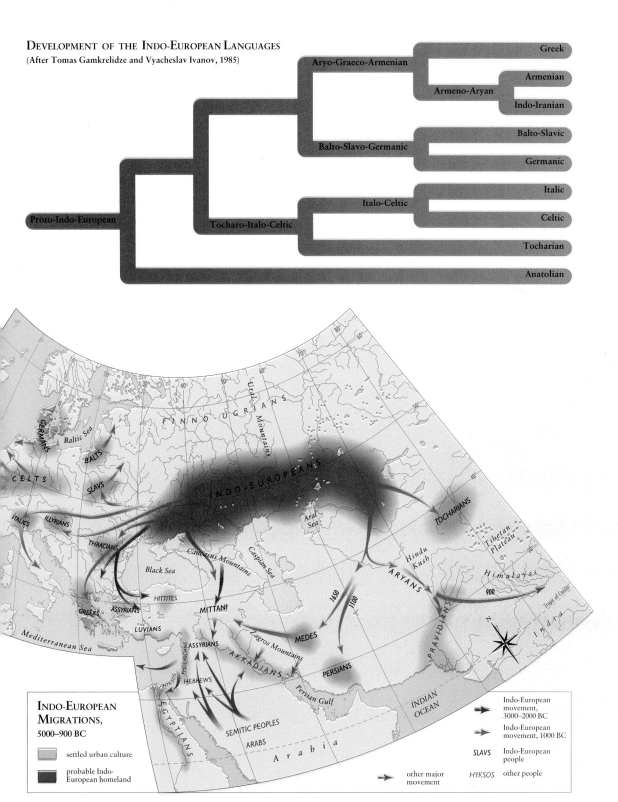

INDO-EUROPEAN
MIGRATIONS,
5000–900 BC

settled urban culture

probable Indo-
European homeland

Indo-European
movement,
3000–2000 BC

Indo-European
movement, 1000 BC

SLAVS   Indo-European
people

HYKSOS   other people

other major
movement

THE PERSIAN EMPIRE UNDER DARIUS I, C. 520 BC

THE ACHAEMENID EMPIRE

Persia at the accession of Cyrus I

extent of the empire under Cyrus "the Great," 559–530 BC

added by Cambyses, 530–522 BC

added by Darius, 521–486 BC

vassal or tributary state or region

Major campaigns of:

Cambyses

Darius

Xerxes

Revolt of Cyrus "the Younger":

march of the "Ten Thousand"

A general in the Persian army and a prince of the Achaemenid dynasty, Darius I "the Great" came to the throne on the death of Cambysis, son of Cyrus "the Great" at a time of revolt in Persia. Darius had been campaigning in Egypt, and it would take him a year to restore peace and establish his authority throughout the empire, by putting down rebellions in the provinces of Babylonia and Susiana.

Darius then turned his attention to the east, winning large areas of northern India and Persia. To further strengthen the Persian frontiers, he invaded Scythia, via the Hellespont. By crossing the Hellespont, Darius had provided a bridge-head into Europe. In 513 BC, he advanced into Greece, subduing eastern Thrace and the Getae and securing Macedonia. He also took the Aegian islands of Lemnos and Imros, although the Persian fleet was later destroyed by a storm near Mount Athos in 492 BC, and the Persian army was defeated by the Athenian general Miltiades at the battle of Marathon in 490 BC. Preparations for a third expedition were halted by

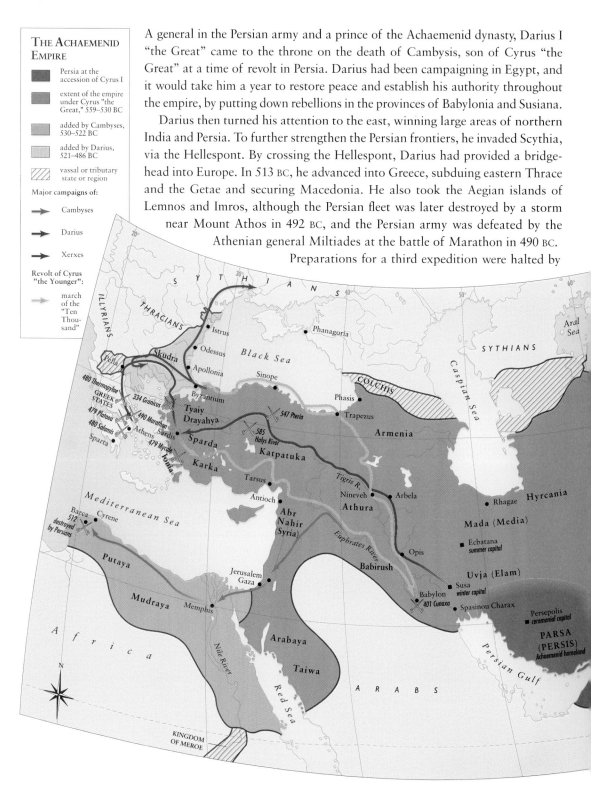

an insurrection in Egypt prior to Darius's death in 486 BC. His Greek campaigns were continued by his son and successor Xerxes (485–465 BC) who, on crushing a rebellion in Egypt and Babylonia, assembled an enormous fleet and crossed the Hellespont, invading Greece. He forced the pass at Thermopylae, defeating Leonidas, King of Sparta, in 480 BC, advancing to occupy Athens for a short time, until his fleet was defeated at Salamis that same year, and his army was defeated at Platae, thus ending Xerxes' ambitions in Greece.

In a shock attack, a poorly armored Persian light-infantry man goes down before an armored Greek hoplite.

Darius had also instrumented a number of building projects, which included a range of fortifications, a canal connecting the Nile with the Red Sea, and the new palace at Susa, which became Darius's administrative capital in 521 BC. Darius was noted for his administrative abilities, whereby he completed the organization of the empire into satrapies, initiated by his predecessor Cyrus "the Great." Darius ordered a land survey to be carried out throughout the Persian empire so that taxes could be levied according to yields. The annual tribute from the provinces helped to stimulate further a flourishing trade and commerce that was also benefiting from opening up new sea routes and the standardization of coinage, weights, and measures.

These policies and developments went hand in hand with a growth in credit banking. Like Cyrus before him, Darius tolerated the religions, practices, beliefs, and institutions of other peoples in his empire, and it can be said that, despite occasional revolts, Persian rule was generally tolerated by the subject peoples.

THE FEUDING STATES OF CHINA, 403–221 BC

Between 722 and 481 BC, the Chou kings gradually lost power and control over China, as central authority and feudal obligations were weakened. Chou power fragmented as new successor states fought against each other over territory in a bid to gain mastery over the Middle Kingdom. There followed a period of constant, large-scale, internecine warfare between both the Chinese kingdoms and barbarian invaders. During this period of conflict seven major states competed against each other: the Han, the Chao, the Wei, the Ch'u, the Yen, the Ch'i, and the Ch'in, of which the main rival were the Ch'u and the Ch'in.

Between 328 and 308 BC, the Ch'in established control over the west and northwest; by 256 BC the royal house of Chou had finally been brought down. Ruling from their heartland, the Ch'in began to expand their territory, annexing their six rival states in turn. They set out to establish a powerful, efficient, and centralized state, aided by the new philosophy of Legalism, which advocated a universal system of law in a centralized state to which all individuals were to be subject. Legalists held that humans were intrinsically selfish; that social order could be maintained only through strong state control and absolute obedience to authority; and that human effort should be directed toward increasing the power of the ruler and the state.

The Ch'in had overcome their rival states by 221 BC, when the ruler

Against the background of anarchy and disorder, Chinese philosophy flourished. Here Chinese sages engage in the Taoist study of the Yin and Yang.

proclaimed himself First Emperor of all China. They set out to improve agriculture, commerce, and industry, built new road systems and extensive irrigation schemes, and unified the systems of currency, economy, defense, law, writing, and even ideology, set against the background of the continuing philosophical development of Confucianism, Taoism, and Legalism.

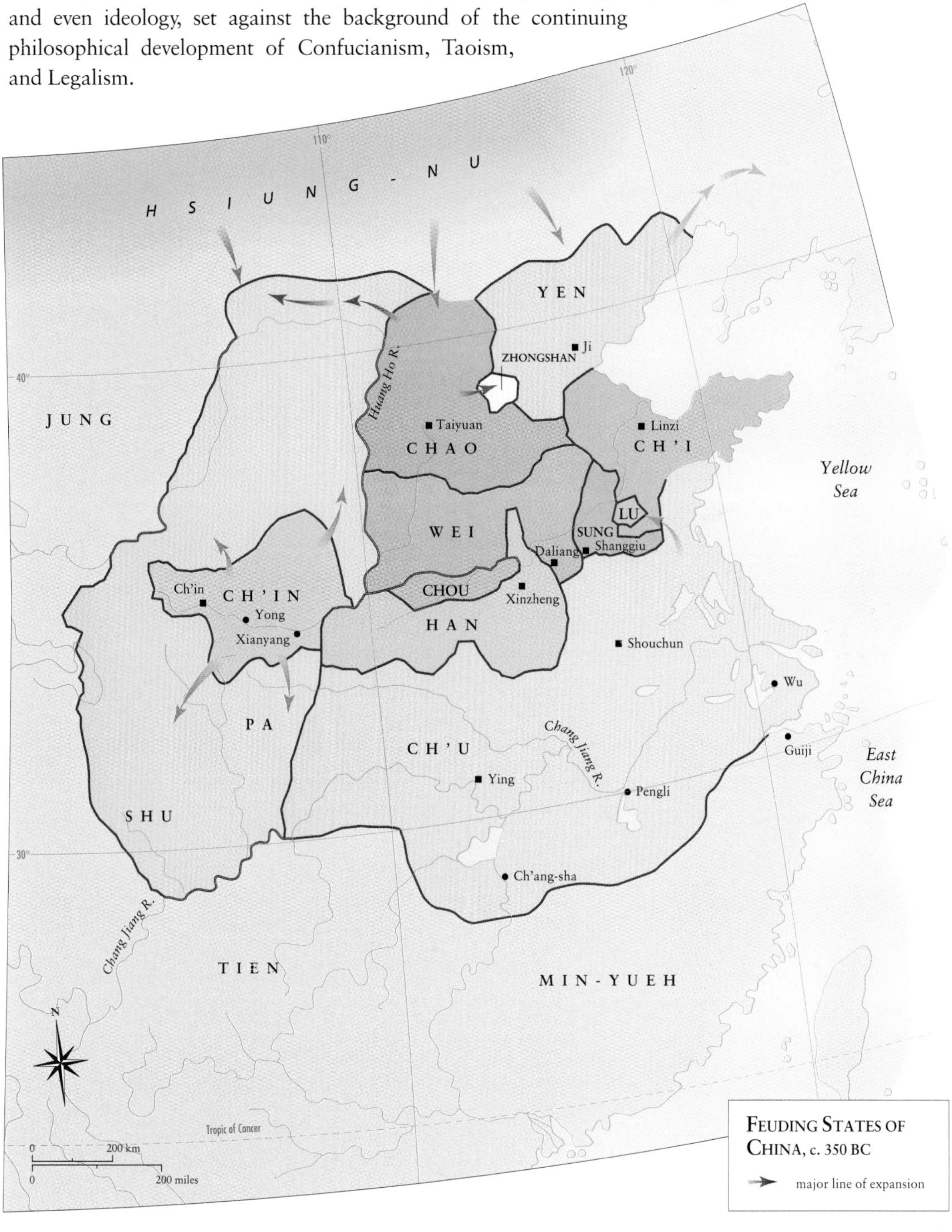

H S I U N G - N U

H S I U N G

YEN

JUNG

ZHONGSHAN ■ Ji

Huang Ho R.

■ Taiyuan
CHAO

■ Linzi
CH'I

Yellow
Sea

WEI

LU

SUNG
Daliang ■ ■ Shanggiu

Ch'in ■
CH'IN
● Yong
Xianyang ●

CHOU
HAN

■ Xinzheng

■ Shouchun

● Wu

PA

CH'U

Chang Jiang R.

● Guiji

East
China
Sea

■ Ying

● Pengli

SHU

Chang Jiang R.

● Ch'ang-sha

N

TIEN

MIN-YUEH

200 km

Tropic of Cancer

0

200 miles
0

**FEUDING STATES OF
CHINA, c. 350 BC**

→   major line of expansion

ALEXANDER'S CAMPAIGNS IN ASIA MINOR

This mosaic shows Alexander, a brilliant military commander, whose personal charisma enabled him to hold together his multi-ethnic empire, which collapsed after his death.

Alexander inherited from his father, Philip II of Macedon, both a large and capable army and a plan to conquer Persia. In the spring of 334 BC, he crossed the Hellespont with 35,000 men. He attacked an army of Persians and Greek mercenaries at the Granicus River, defeating it with little loss to his own forces. His victory ensured the eventual submission of all the states in Asia Minor. Alexander refused to engage the substantial Persian fleet and resolved to defeat it by occupying all coastal cities and ports in the Persian empire. Accordingly, after reducing Lycian and Pisidian hill tribes in western Asia Minor, he advanced southward and soon met Darius and the main Persian army in north-eastern Syria at Issus (333 BC). Macedonian pikemen punched a hole through the Persian forces, generating a complete rout, turned into a disaster by the relentless pursuit of Alexander's cavalry. After capturing

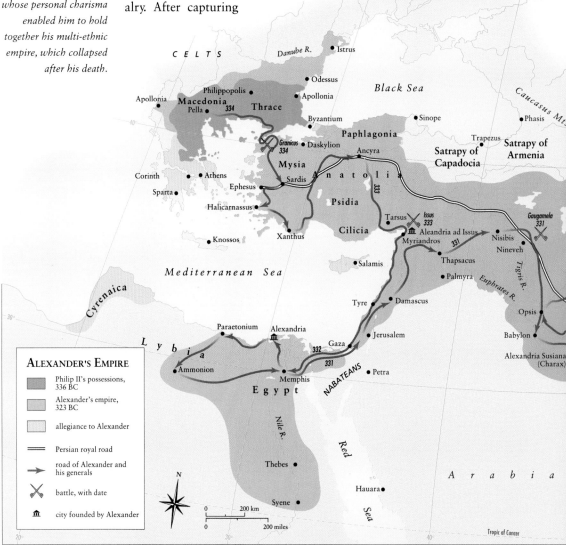

ALEXANDER'S EMPIRE

Philip II's possessions, 336 BC

Alexander's empire, 323 BC

allegiance to Alexander

Persian royal road

road of Alexander and his generals

battle, with date

city founded by Alexander

Darius's family, which he treated with respect, Alexander marched south to Syria and Phoenicia, and moved into Egypt, thus securing control of the whole eastern Mediterranean and ensuring strategic control at sea. On the Nile estuary, Alexander founded Alexandria, which became a center for science, philosophy, and trade. Alexander moved north to attack Babylon. Crossing the Euphrates and Tigris, he again met Darius, completely defeating him at Gaugamela (331 BC). Darius fled and was eventually murdered by his own generals. When Alexander reached Persepolis, the Persian capital, he burned Xerxes' palace in revenge for the destruction of the Acropolis in 480 BC. With Darius dead, Alexander could legitimately claim to be the Great King. He only needed to gain the submission of the Persian satraps. His empire now extended beyond the Caspian Sea to present-day Afghanistan and Baluchistan and northward to Bactria and Sogdiana. Thinking to acquire the remaining oddments of the Persian empire, Alexander crossed the Indus and fought his last great battle on the Hydaspes against the kingdom of Porus (in the Punjab). When his troops mutinied and refused to go any farther, Alexander followed the Indus to the Arabian Sea and arrived in Babylon in 323 BC. In the summer of that year, he died of fever. Alexander achieved much militarily, but he totally failed to organize his empire. No provision was made for his succession.

> "The end and object of conquest is to avoid doing the same thing as the conquered."
> *Alexander the Great*

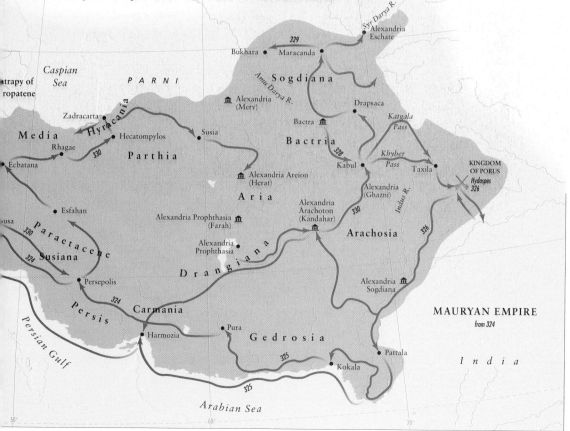

ALEXANDER'S SUCCESSORS

On Alexander's death in 323 BC, a few days before his thirty-third birthday, his sprawling empire almost immediately began to fall apart.

Antigonus, the most powerful of Alexander's generals, initially seized power, but he did not go unchallenged for long, eventually being defeated by his most determined rival, Seleucus I. After a further two decades of warfare with various contenders, Seleucus became master of an empire that reached from the Mediterranean Sea to the Indus River.

Perhaps the most successful of Alexander's inheritors, Ptolemy seized and ruled Egypt, founding a dynasty whose administration was firmly established in Greek or Macedonian hands; all major district officials and army officers were Greek. It is said that Cleopatra, the last of the dynasty, was the first to learn the Egyptian language.

Meanwhile in Macedonia, Alexander's homeland, possession of the territory was won by a hard fought contest. By 276 Antigonus Gonatus succeeded

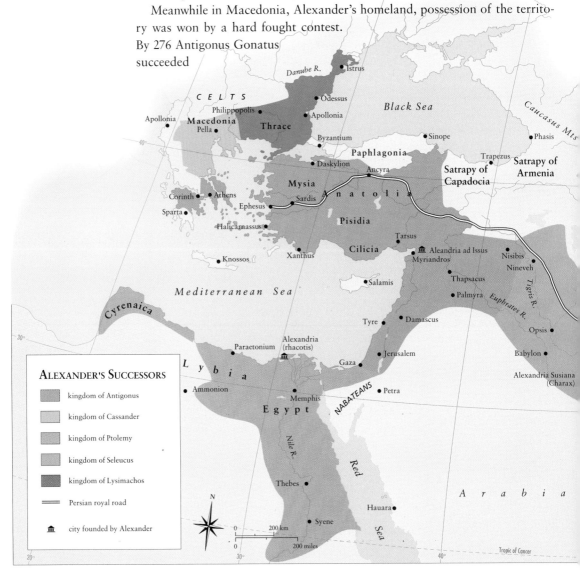

ALEXANDER'S SUCCESSORS

- kingdom of Antigonus
- kingdom of Cassander
- kingdom of Ptolemy
- kingdom of Seleucus
- kingdom of Lysimachos
- Persian royal road
- 🏛 city founded by Alexander

in vanquishing his contenders, and he created a dynasty, which would last until Macedonia was conquered by Rome in 168 BC.

The Seleucid empire, the largest successor state, attained its greatest power under Antiochus III, acquiring Armenia and invading Parthia, which had grown from the nomadic Parni under Arsaces I. An alliance with the Graeco-Bactrian state (established under Diodotus I) followed; eventually, Antiochus gained Palestine and southern Asia Minor. Antiochus III interfered in Macedonian affairs and was confronted by an expanionist Roman state. His fleet was defeated at Myonnesus (190), and he himself was beaten at Magnesia (190) in Asia Minor. The resultant Peace of Apameia forced Antiochus to surrender Asia Minor west of the Taurus Mountains, which was then divided between Rhodes and Pergamon. Taking advantage of Seleucid weakness, Armenia threw off its chains under the leadership of Artaxias, as did Bactria, which survived as a Hellenestic state until invaded by the Yue-Chi and Sakas. After the death of Antiochus, the Seleucid state was weakened by a series of wars against Egypt and Parthia. During this period, the Jews under Judas Maccabeus rebelled and created the Hasmonean state that was eventually annexed by Rome. Between 95–64 BC, murder and treachery destoyed the last vestiges of coherence in the ruling family, and in 64, Pompey made Syria, the Seleucid remnant, into a Roman province.

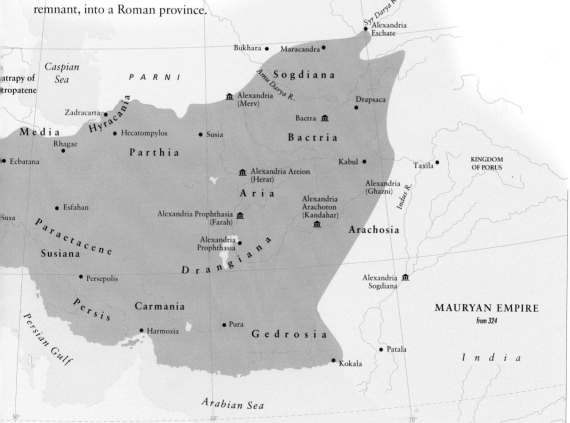

PART II: COMMUNICATION, COMMERCE, AND CULTURE

In AD 90, an anonymous Egyptian-Greek author, probably from Berenice on the Red Sea coast, wrote a navigational manual, *Periplus Maris Erythreae* (Navigation of the Indian Ocean). He described Indian market towns on the Malabar Coast, mentioning Pondicherry and Madras, and Ceylon. The Ganges River was characterized as a trading center for spikenard, pearls, and muslins and was linked to Bactria by an overland trade route down which came raw silk, silk yarn, and silk cloth from China. The Malay Peninsula was reputed to have the best tortoiseshell in the Indian Ocean. *The Hou Han Shou*, the annals of the younger Han dynasty, recount how musicians and jesters from Rome arrived in about AD 120 and performed in front of the Han emperor. Such descriptions suggest that ties of trade had existed for many years within Asia and between Asia and the Mediterranean world.

As Islam established itself along the Silk Road, mosques were built for travelers and local converts, some of which exist to this day. This mosque is found in the Sinkiang province in China and reveals the continuing force of Islam in central Asia.

East and South Asia remained virtually unknown in the Middle East until the Achaemenians under Cyrus II gained control of Persia in the sixth century BC. His son-in-law Darius subjugated the Indus River region in 513 BC. The Persian empire was tied together by royal roads. A continuous series of rest house stations linked Sardis, on the Aegean coast with Susa, the capital—1,600 miles away. However, centuries before the Persian empire, the Chinese possessed a fully developed road system built and maintained by a highways organization. Economic and cultural contacts developed from the first century AD. The

Periplus Maris Erythreae indicated that Petra in contemporary Jordan linked Red Sea routes with those of western Asia. Indian copper, sandalwood, teak, and ebony were shipped to the Arabian Gulf, in return for pearls, textiles, wine, dates, gold, and slaves. The Indus Delta ports imported linen, topaz, coral, frankincense, glass, silver, and wine, while Broach in the Gulf of Cambay was the major transit port on the northwestern part of the Indian coast, handling most of the trade with western Asia, Italy, Greece, and Arabia. Broach exported spices, jewels, and tortoiseshell. Trade routes then proceeded around the tip of southern India and up the coast to the eastern ports. One such, Arikamedu, contained a Roman trading station. Archaeological evidence suggests the Romans used the port from the first century BC to the early second century AD. Finds including Roman pottery, beads, glass, terra-cotta, and Roman gold coin hoards have been found in the Deccan. The coins are from the time of Augustus and Tiberias. For a time, Roman trade with India was so great that Pliny the Elder complained that India was draining Roman gold reserves. Sea routes then continued to the Malay Peninsula and the Indonesian Islands; traders searched for spices for the Roman market.

In northern India, Taxila was a transit city collecting turquoise and lapis lazuli from Persia and Afghanistan, and silk came along the Silk Road from China. During Rome's conflict with Parthia, the Parthians stopped Chinese goods from reaching the West directly; this trade was diverted via Taxila, adding to the wealth of northern India.

More difficult trade routes were those crossing the deserts of western Asia from Arabian Gulf ports. The city of Palmyra organized and escorted trade caravans just as Petra handled goods arriving in the Red Sea. The most spectacular road was the Silk Road, leaving Tun-huang and dividing into northern and southern routes around the Takla Makan desert rejoining at Kashgar to reach Tashkent, Kokand, Samarkand, and Merv. There Greek, Arab, Roman, Indian, and Iranian traders exchanged goods with nomad traders, who undertook the middle part of the journey. This period also saw Indian culture spreading to southeast Asia as trade developed with China.

During the first and second centuries AD, a new dynasty combining the Yueh-chi and the Tocharians established the vast Kushan empire, extending from northern India into central Asia. The Kushans were instrumental in spreading Buddhism along the Silk Road, converting the central Asian oasis towns and finally exporting Buddhism into China. Some Silk Road towns comprised mainly Buddhist monasteries and stupas (ritual centers of monasteries). After the fourth century, cave temples were cut into cliffs in central Asia and painted with murals and decorated with religious images. At Tun-huang there are about 460 caves filled with images. Kushans were also important in the development of Mahayana Buddhism. This Buddhist link cemented cultural relations between India and China, and by AD 300, Chinese Buddhists had been traveling to central Asia to study Buddhism. One Chinese pilgrim, Fa-hsien, traveled to and lived in India from about AD 399 to 414. His travel diary makes it clear that

This is a detail from the temple of Borobudur, part of a vast Buddhist complex in Java.

Buddhism was, by this date, in decline in India, although it continued to flourish in southeast Asia, Ceylon, Korea, and Japan.

The importance of religion must not be underrated. Buddhism introduced Indian culture into many parts of Asia, with local rulers endowing monasteries. Indian scripts were adopted, and many Indians settled in central Asia and Afghanistan. During the T'ang period (AD 618–907), Indian traders lived in Canton. In the eighth century, an Indian monk visited Japan to find Japanese Buddhists who were familiar with an Indian alphabet.

Roman trade had developed in turn Indian commerce with southeast Asia, but after the Romans conquered Parthia, Roman trade declined, so the southeast trade assumed greater importance, and Indian culture infiltrated societies in present Thailand, Cambodia, and Laos. Indian settlements spread to the Mekong Delta and the Malay Peninsula; ships sailed to Burma and Indonesia. The cultural impact was immense—Hindus and Buddhists traded and settled, merging Indian civilization with local cultures in a variety of ways. However, historians dispute the numbers of Indians involved. Rather than assuming large Indian colonies abroad, more recent scholarship suggests Buddhists and Hindu Brahmins (high-caste Hindus) acquired positions of influence and used these to instil their beliefs and culture locally. During the fourth century AD, Sanskrit inscriptions were used in Funan, and excavations at the Cambodian town of Oc Eo reveal evidence of Indian architecture. Eventually, the area became part of the Khmer state of Cambodia. Likewise, the Malay Peninsula reveals a number of Indianized states during the third century AD; Tun Sun had more than five hundred Indian merchants and priests. In Burma, the Mons blended Indian culture with their own by molding their animistic religious beliefs with Theravada Buddhism, by adopting Hindu coronation rituals, and by initially building stupas on an Indian model.

Asia, in common with Europe, faced a major crisis when mounted nomads poured out of the northeastern steppes. These loosely federated tribes spoke a variant of Turkish and fought in a fashion that was difficult to combat. They made composite bows of bone, horn, and wood and fought as mounted archers, seldom coming to close quarters but then using the saber. One large group, known as the Hsiung-nu, lived outside the Great Wall of China. Their power was broken by the Han using similar cavalry tactics; their remnants moved to central Asia, where they federated with Iranian nomads and Siberian Mongol tribes. Other Mongolian tribes broke into China in the fourth century AD, setting up an independent state in Shensi and Shansi in northern China. A powerful Turkish people, the Toba, invaded and succeeded in reuniting northern China, but they adopted Chinese culture, customs, and language, creating a new Sinicized nomadic aristocracy, and this group supplied membership of the Sui (581–617) and T'ang (618–907) dynasties.

In AD 480, the White Huns invaded India and destroyed the remnants of the Gupta empire. Despite being expelled, they returned in about AD 500 and terrorized western India for a generation, before finally being pushed back into

"If you were to ask me why I dwell among green mountains, I should laugh silently; my soul is serene. The peach blossom follows the moving water; There is another heaven and earth beyond the world of man."
Li Po (701–762), T'ang dynasty poet

Kashmir. In about AD 430, Varahran V of the Sasanid empire attacked and defeated other tribes of the White Huns near the Oxus River, but they kept on coming back. Sometimes they allied with members of the Sasanid ruling house seeking to usurp the throne. They were finally defeated in AD 554. The White Huns are represented in Byzantine sources and on Indian coins as a white race from central Asia. Historians now suggest that the term Hun is not a term of ethnicity, but is political. In eastern Asia, successors of the Hsiung-nu, the Blue Turks, created an empire from Manchuria to the Syr Darya River in central Asia. Their pressure decanted other Turkic tribes westward where, after amalgamating with other nomads, they appeared in Hungary as the Avars, building an empire from the fifth to the eighth centuries.

The next major onslaught in Asia came during the spread of Islam. When Mohammed died in 632, Muslim power had spread through the Hejaz and most of central and southern Arabia. Within one hundred years, Arab forces took Anatolia, the Fertile Crescent, Persia, and Afghanistan, and Sind in India fell in 712. This new world power contained people of different origins and religions; nevertheless, a coherent Arab culture rapidly developed. Islam and Arabic soon predominated; the fact that the Koran was banned from translation aided this process. Subject peoples were allowed to pursue their own religion and were free from persuasion or conversion to Islam but were taxed. Tensions did emerge between non-tax-paying warriors and subjects who had converted to Islam. Also, non-Arabs desired equality, and this was granted, the process being helped by the removal of the capital to Damascus, then Baghdad, thereby reducing Arabs and Arabia in importance.

The Arabs cut the European trade routes to India, pushing their way into the Caucasus, east of the Caspian, to the Aral Sea and the Jaxartes, and the mouth of the Indus. The Mediterranean became the boundary between different people and cultures, between Christian Europe and the Muslim world. However, trade did continue with India and China. Trading stations were set up in India, Ceylon, the Malay Peninsula, Sumatra, and southern China. Arab dhows sailed the Indian Ocean using the monsoon winds, and Chinese junks, sailing westward, had begun to appear west of India before Mohammed. In 875, in the city of Hangchou, it is recorded that 26,000 foreigners were slaughtered when the Chinese turned against them during a civil war. After this, Arabs went no farther than Kalah, their station on the Malay Peninsula, and Galle in Ceylon. Exports to the West included cinnamon, ginger, nutmeg, and cloves from Molucca. Other goods were camphor, aloes, incense, musk, and ambergris. The prices of these wares reached such a proportion that western exports of wood, hemp, tar, lead, iron, furs, wool, olive oil, and almonds could no longer cover the cost and the balance had to be paid in gold.

In cultural terms, the Arabs used Asian and Hellenistic legacies. Centers of learning were established at Baghdad, Damascus, Cairo, Mecca, and Samarkand. The Abbasid caliphate encouraged arts and sciences. Hindu scientific works, the *Sidhantas, Charaka,* and *Sustrata,* were translated into

Arabic. Jabir recorded chemical methods, techniques, and apparatus, the refining of metals, the distillation of alcohol, and glassmaking. A chemistry school developed, and a body of writings on chemistry emerged.

After the battle of Talas in 751, between Arabs and Chinese, prisoners taught the Arabs how to make paper, and this spread rapidly around the Arab world. A house of knowledge was established in Baghdad, holding transcripts of philosophical, literary, and scientific works translated from Greek, Syriac, Persian, and Sanskrit. Scholarly translations provided commentaries on Aristotle, and Hunayn Ibn-Ishaq (c. 809–877) translated the works of the Greek physician Galen and some of those of Ptolemy and Hippocrates. Al-Farghani set up an astronomical observatory; he died around 850, his work being continued by Al-Battani (c. 858–929) and Thabit Ibn-Quarra (c. 826–901), who also translated Greek mathematical and physical texts (Apollonius, Euclid, Ptolemy). Al-Khwarizmi introduced Hindu numerals and methods of calculation to the Arab world. Al-Rhazi was a physician and an encyclopedist who added his thoughts on gynecology, obstetrics, and ophthalmic surgery, while Ibn-Sina wrote on medicine. Many of these works were later translated into Latin and underpinned the Age of the Enlightenment in Europe during the eighteenth century.

Wooden tower pagodas were built from the third century onward. The Shija pagoda, part of the Buddhist palace complex, built around 1056, is the only wooden building of its type that has survived in China. It is 220 feet high (67 meters) and 86 feet in diameter (26 meters).

THE MAURYAN EMPIRE IN INDIA, C. 322 BC

The Mauryan empire was founded by Chandragupta (a regional military commander, c. 321–297 BC), who raised a rebellion and seized control of the kingdom of Magadha. Taking advantage of Alexander the Great's death, he wrenched the Punjab from Macedonian forces and then extended his control over most of the Indian subcontinent, with his capital at Pataliputra (Patna). Threatened by Chandragupta's growing power, Seleucis of Syria, Alexander's successor, challenged him by invading northern India in 305 BC but suffered a devastating defeat. A treaty ending the conflict gave Chandragupta all lands north to the Hindu Kush, including Baluchistan and Afghanistan. Chandragupta used an extensive and elaborate civil service, an army, and a secret service to rule. A virtual dictatorship coincided with widespread public works, building roads and developing irrigation systems. Chandragupta's chief minister was Kautilya, who wrote about law and government in the *Arthasastra*. Six stages of diplomacy were analyzed: neutrality, friendship, alliance, deception, hostility, and war; in sophistication and philosophy, Kautilya's opus rivals Machiavelli's cunning treatise on statecraft, *The Prince*.

The Mauryan dynasty's greatest ruler was Asoka, Chandragupta's grandson. He came to the throne after fighting his brothers for the succession. His policy was to continue enlarging the empire, and in 251 BC, he invaded and conquered Kalinga, part of modern Andhra Pradesh, Orissa, and Madhya Pradesh. The Kalinga campaign caused such extensive misery and destruction to the local population that Asoka renounced armed conquest and adopted a policy of "conquest by dharma," by spiritual rectitude and law. Asoka spent the rest of his life patronizing Buddhism but did not suppress the traditional Hindu religion followed by many people. Asoka decided to teach Buddhist principles to his subjects, and his sayings were made known by engravings and inscriptions on rocks and pillars at suitable sites. The Rock Edicts and Pillar Edicts publicized statements regarding his thoughts and actions. Asoka sought to spread virtues of honesty, truthfulness, compassion, mercy, nonviolence, nonextravagance, nonacquisitiveness, and kindness to animals; this included the building of animal hospitals. He practiced what he preached and also became a vegetarian. He built many Buddhist shrines, such as the Great Stupa of Sanchi, and exhorted people of all faiths to respect other creeds and refrain from adversely criticizing the viewpoints of others. As part of his religious campaign, he sent Buddhist missionaries to Syria, Egypt, Greece, Macedonia, and Epirus, without much success, but achieved much more in Burma and Ceylon. Other good works were the founding of hospitals, increasing the supply of medicines, providing roadside shade by planting trees and groves, and building rest houses. The Mauryan empire did not survive long after Asoka's death in 232 BC. His sons divided the empire, and its power declined; the northwest went to Bactrian Greeks by about 180 BC. Other dynasties quickly appeared, the longest-lived being the Sunga. This time was a time of persecution and decline of Buddhism in India, and led to the triumph of Brahmin Hinduism. Finally, northern India succumbed to foreign invaders such as the Yue-chi and Sakas, who pushed India into chaos.

Asoka sought to spread his beliefs on kingship and humanitarian virtues by erecting pillar edicts, such as this sandstone pillar, engraved with his philosophy.

THE UNIFICATION OF CHINA

"A state where uniformity of purpose has been established for ten years, will be strong for a hundred years; for a hundred years it will be strong for a thousand years."
Lord Shang, Ch'in official

Once the Ch'in dynasty (221–206 BC) had conquered their rivals, they set out to unify China by creating a powerful centralized state. The old kingdoms were broken up and replaced by new administrative districts within different boundaries, which in turn were controlled by thirty-six (and later forty-two) commandaries, each with a military and civil governor and an advisor. Local customs were destroyed and language reforms took place, in order to harmonize understanding between different regions by diminishing regional difference; meanwhile the centralized authority of the Ch'in was legitimized by the new philosophy of Legalism. Further centralist measures took place, as uniform weights and measures were introduced. In 213 BC, the Legalist Li Su advocated the burning of all books held in private libraries, in a further bid to stamp out local differences and opposition. This act proved to be a terrible loss to early Chinese culture, worsened by the fact that many scholars were executed in this purge.

Shih Huang-ti (221–209 BC) became the first ruler to call himself emperor, and he established an imperial system that would last for two thousand years. He abolished feudalism, replacing the feudal hierarchy by a bureaucratic centralized administration, and he had the Great Wall built in 221 BC to protect China from external enemies. The wall spread for 1,400 miles, from the Kansu frontier to the sea. It was built with great loss of life by work gangs of forced laborers and prisoners working in harsh conditions.

The Ch'in dynasty was short-lived, yet it marked a turning point in Chinese history, since the type of nonhereditary bureaucratic government established and developed during the Ch'in period, under an autocratic emperor, became the model for future Chinese political organization for the next two thousand years.

The Ch'in were now confronted with two threats: the continued intrigues of powerful families, said to have numbered 120,000, from the deposed aristocracy of the old feudal states; and the threat of the Hsiung-nu nomads beyond the northern frontier. The suspect families were treated harshly, with the transportation of the nobility to Shensi in the west and the abolition of their feudal holdings, thus giving greater rights and land ownership to their traditional supporters, the peasantry.

The Hsiung-nu empire in central Asia and Mongolia extended from Korea to the Altai and from the Chinese border to north of the great inland sea, Lake Baykal. It would continue to rival the Ch'in and their successors, the Han. Although some historians have interpreted the Hsiung-nu as proto-Huns, this issue has been much debated by historians, since it is likely that the Huns were more a mixture of peoples than a single ethnic entity.

The Ch'in also led military expeditions in the south between 221 and 214 BC against the Vietnamese, Thai, and Khmer of South Yüeh, conquering much of present-day northern Vietnam.

The Ch'in dynasty amalgamated many defensive walls to form the Great Wall of China, which proved of little value in preventing foreign incursions.

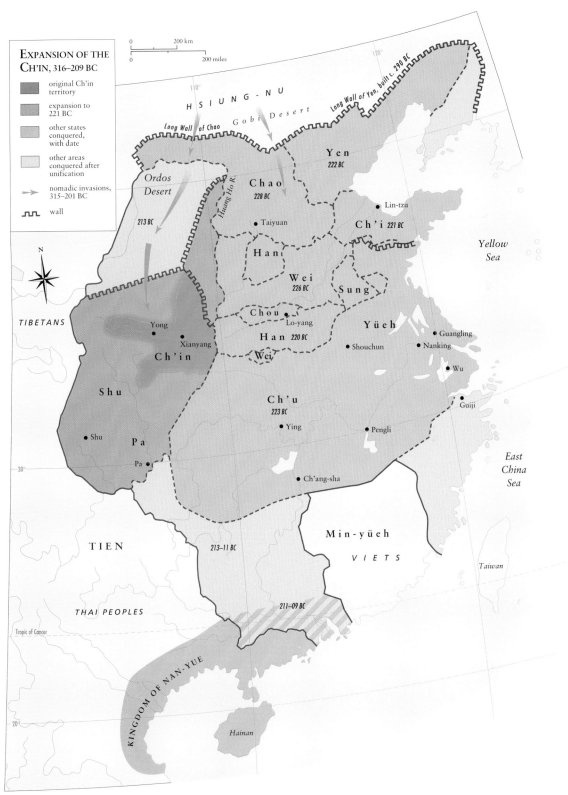

EXPANSION OF THE
CH'IN, 316–209 BC

- original Ch'in territory
- expansion to 221 BC
- other states conquered, with date
- other areas conquered after unification
- nomadic invasions, 315–201 BC
- wall

200 km
200 miles

HSIUNG-NU

Gobi Desert

Long Wall of Yen, built c. 290 BC

Long Wall of Chao

Ordos Desert

Huang Ho R.

Yen
222 BC

Chao
228 BC

213 BC

Taiyuan

Lin-tzu

Ch'i 221 BC

Han

Wei
226 BC

Sung

Yellow Sea

TIBETANS

Yong

Xianyang

Ch'in

Chou

Lo-yang

Han 220 BC

Wei

Yüeh

Shouchun

Guangling

Nanking

Wu

Shu

Pa

Shu

Pa

Ch'u
223 BC

Ying

Pengli

Guiji

East China Sea

Ch'ang-sha

Min-yüeh

213–11 BC

VIETS

Taiwan

TIEN

THAI PEOPLES

211–09 BC

Tropic of Cancer

KINGDOM OF NAN-YUE

Hainan

THE SILK ROAD, C. 112 BC

During the period of Han expansion, between 140 and 87 BC, offensives against the Hsiung-nu resulted in the conquest of present-day Sinkiang, and the extension of the Great Wall farther to the northwest. This meant that the Chinese now controlled and protected the main trade route into central Asia. Subsequent missions sent into Parthia and Bactria led to considerable increase in trade with the West.

The Silk Road was the caravan trade route that crossed Asia into Asia Minor and the Mediterranean littoral. The route originated in Lin-tzu on the Yellow Sea and stretched for 4,000 miles to the Mediterranean Sea, with two routes that bypassed either to the north or south of the Takla-Makan desert, north via Karashahr and Aksu and south via Cherchen and Yarkand; the route then climbed the Pamirs into Afghanistan, and trailed across Persia to Antioch, in Syria, with offshoots from Bactria to Turkestan and India. It linked ancient China with the West, especially Rome, and later with

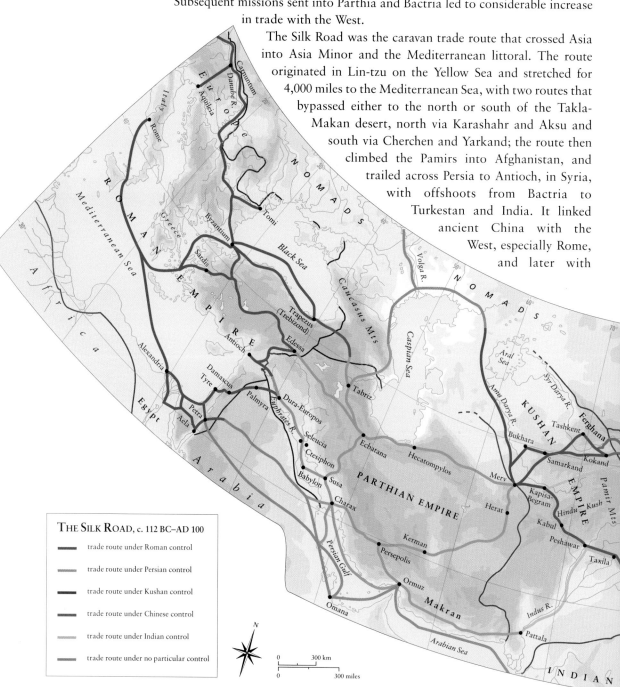

THE SILK ROAD, c. 112 BC–AD 100

- trade route under Roman control
- trade route under Persian control
- trade route under Kushan control
- trade route under Chinese control
- trade route under Indian control
- trade route under no particular control

Byzantium. Goods were normally handled in different stages by middlemen, rather than individuals or caravanserai, who traveled the whole route. Silk cloth, the main export item, traveled one way into Europe, while wool, gold, silver, and other luxurious goods went East. The Silk Road implied not only a transfer of merchandise, but also the exchange of ideas, religions, philosophies, and art between East and West. China would gain Buddhism from India and Nestorian Christianity from the Middle East.

Later, in AD 97, Pan Chao led an expedition across the Pamirs, with the intention of establishing a direct contact with the Roman empire. Although he failed in his mission, he nevertheless got as far as the Caspian Sea, the farthest point ever reached by the Chinese in their westward expansion. This expedition also confirmed Chinese control over much of the Silk Road.

Much later, with the decline of the Western Roman empire and the rise of Byzantium, Constantinople would serve as an entrepôt and halfway house of the main trade route between Europe and Asia. Under the control of Greek and Syrian merchants, trade with China and India enriched the Byzantine empire, although this trade depended much upon a working relationship with Persian merchants, the main enemy of Byzantium throughout most of the sixth and the first half of the seventh century; consequently, trade would often be suspended during the wars between Byzantium and the Sasanid empire.

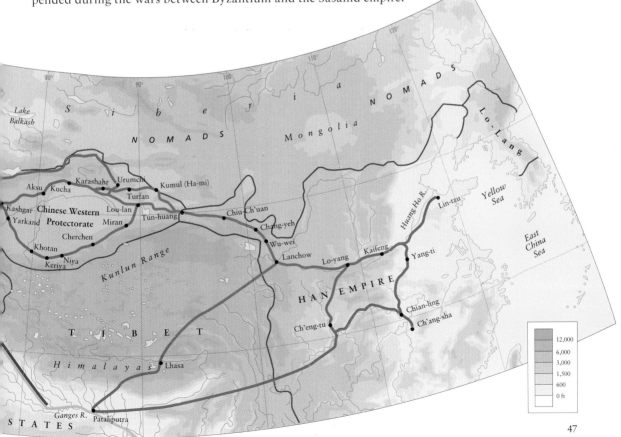

THE HAN DYNASTY IN CHINA

This portrayal of a Han chariot in battle array demonstrates their attempts to match the mobility of the nomads.

Draconic laws, heavy taxation, and thousands of deaths among the work gangs on the northern frontier led to widespread discontent in China, as peasant rebellions broke out, one after another, against the despotic Ch'in dynasty. Ch'in rule collapsed into a state of chaos and anarchy throughout most of eastern and southern China. In the ensuing struggle with the last Ch'in emperor, Hsiang Yü, Liu Pang rose to power.

Liu Pang, posthumously known as Han Kao-tzu (207–195 BC), was the first ruler of the Han dynasty, which maintained power until AD 220, with the exception of the short interlude between AD 9 and 25, otherwise known as the usurpation of Wang Mang. The Han dynasty brought to China a period of comparative stability, based on compromise, in contradistinction to the repression of the Ch'in dynasty. The Han were to be the longest reigning of Chinese dynasties that could claim to be a single and true authority in China.

In 119 BC, under Emperor Han Wu-ti (c. 141–86 BC), the Han extended power against the Viet (Yüeh) tribes into the Gulf of Tonking on the South China Sea, and they would spread Chinese civilization to Korea by 109 BC.

The northern frontier remained a constant concern. By 119 BC, Han Wu-ti had pushed the nomadic Hsiung-nu beyond the Gobi desert. Meanwhile, a Chinese mission penetrating westward discovered the Greco-Buddhist kingdom of Bactria. They found that the Bactrians were utilizing much larger horses in their cavalry force than the Mongolian ponies employed by the Hsiung-nu. Taking advantage of this, they developed a more heavily armed cavalry; they were able to defeat the Hsiung-nu in combat. However, in 58 BC the Hsiung-nu empire collapsed due to internal rifts, so that it would no longer be a threat to the Chinese state.

The Han brought prosperity to China, with economic,

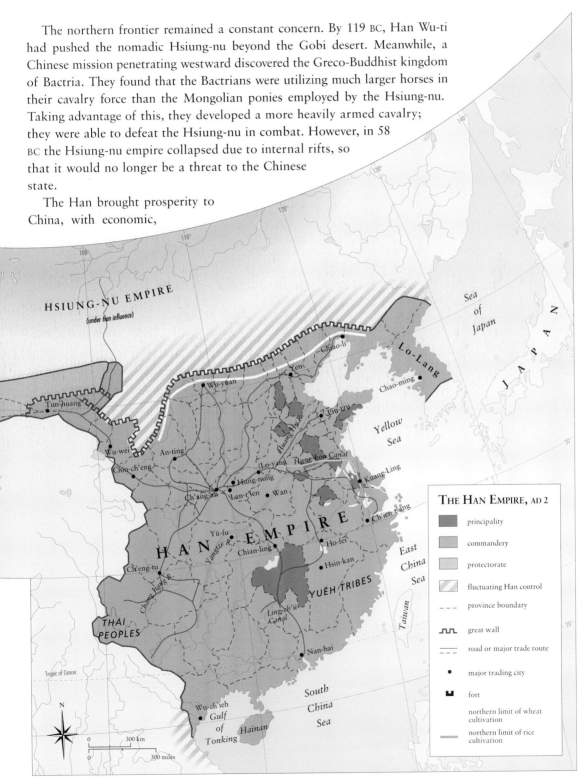

THE HAN EMPIRE, AD 2

- principality
- commandery
- protectorate
- fluctuating Han control
- province boundary
- great wall
- road or major trade route
- major trading city
- fort
- northern limit of wheat cultivation
- northern limit of rice cultivation

"The Western capital lies in sad confusion; The wolf and tiger come to plague the people. Whitened bones were strewn across the plain."
Poet *Wang Ts'an*, reflecting on the effects of revolution

administrative, and cultural reforms, inheriting from the Ch'in, the foundations of Chinese unity. This was bolstered by a civil service made of Confucian scholars, whose recruitment was regulated by examinations. These were introduced by Han Wu-ti in 130 BC; they proved to be the forerunner of a system that would be regulated under the T'ang in the seventh century AD. An imperial university was founded in 124 BC.

The Han expanded the road and canal systems in a climate of improving technology that witnessed the invention of paper. Agriculture developed, aided by a growth in irrigation schemes and the greater use of iron tools.

Due to a succession of child emperors, by the middle of the second century the Han state went into gradual decline that was accompanied by factional disputes and court intrigues. The situation was exacerbated by tensions with the Chi'ang tribes in the northwest and by a distressed rural population who expressed their grievances in the uprising in 184. In 220, the last Han emperor, Hsien-ti (189–220), abdicated, and the empire was divided into three independent states, the Three Kingdoms, remaining politically fragmented until 589. In the meantime China fell victim to numerous non-Chinese invaders and the personal ambitions of individual Chinese warlords.

As the Han empire went into decline, even the rural heartlands, such as Guilin (shown here in modern day), suffered from the effects of maladministration and division.

A pottery model of a sheep pen from the Han period.

KHITANS

JUAN-JUAN

HSIEN-PI

YU

KOGURYO

Kungnaesong

Sea of Japan

TOBA

Xianping

Lo-lang

SILLA

Kyongju

Ikaruga

Asuka

Gobi Desert

Pincheng

WEI

Huang Ho R.

Ji'nan

PAENCHE

Karak

YAMATA KINGDOM

Yellow Sea

TIBETANS

Doughai

Lo-yang

Hung-kou Canal

Qin

Nanyang

Nanjing

SHU

Yangtze R.

Hangchou

Ch'eng-tu

Pa

Jiangling

Yuchan

East China Sea

Chang Jiang R.

Tanchou

WU

Taiwan

Ling-ch'ü Canal

THAI KINGDOMS

Canton

Tropic of Cancer

VIETS

South China Sea

Hainan

0   300 km

0   300 miles

N

THREE KINGDOMS, 264

Wei kingdom, c. 240

Shu kingdom, c. 240

Wu kingdom, c. 240

Great Wall

Wei conquest of Shu, 263

Shu refugees flee Wei conquest to Persia, 263–64

Thai kingdoms, with varying dates of independence, c. 300

51

THE SASANIAN EMPIRE

The Sasanids were an ancient Iranian dynasty who saw themselves as successors to the Archaemenids when they overthrew the Parthians in Iran in AD 226. The Sasanid dynasty began with Adashir I (AD 208–241) and lasted until its destruction by the Arabs between 637 and 651. The Sasanids created a powerful and highly centralized state, based upon central government and provincial officials, with the government taking responsibility for financing roadbuilding, urban development, and agriculture.

Adashir, an excellent but ruthless general, came to power, taking the crown of Persis in 208, then conquering Kerman and the coastal lands of the Persian Gulf, followed by the conquest of Isfahan, Elymais, and Mesene in western Iran. Once he had defeated the Parthians at Hormizdagan in 224, he established his capital in the former Parthian capital of Ctesiphon, in Mesopotamia. Then, as "King of Kings," he was able to consolidate power as leader of the Sasanian empire. Adashir built many cities and was renowned for his building projects, a role that would be continued by his son, Shapur I (241–272).

Despite the constantly changing frontiers

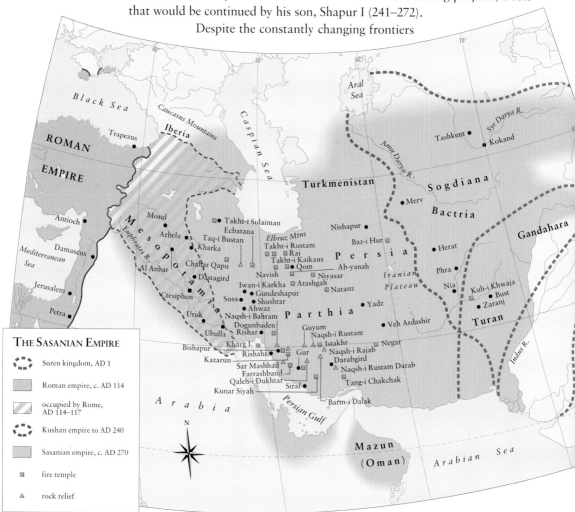

THE SASANIAN EMPIRE

- Suren kingdom, AD 1
- Roman empire, c. AD 114
- occupied by Rome, AD 114–117
- Kushan empire to AD 240
- Sasanian empire, c. AD 270
- ▪ fire temple
- △ rock relief

This rock relief from Nagsh-i Rus Van depicts Ardeshir I, founder of the Sasanid dynasty, facing a hostile Parthian.

of empire, the Sasanids gradually extended their rule over Persia and throughout Mesopotamia, Bactria, Armenia, and Turkmenistan between 224 and 265. Sasanian armies continued their advance, with forces made up of heavy cavalry, supported by elephants and light cavalry. Their rule stretched from the Tigris and Euphrates in the west to the Indus Valley and the Oxus River in the east, and from the Aral and Caspian Seas in the north to the Arabian Sea and the Persian Gulf in the south. The Sasanian empire overthrew the Kushan empire in the east and began to pose a serious threat to the Roman empire in the west, when, in 244, the Sasanids under Shapur I defeated Gordian III on the Euphrates. By 272, the Sasanids had conquered much of Syria from the Romans, capturing the Roman emperor, Valerian, in the process.

Shapur I, who saw himself as the equal of his predecessors Cyrus and Darius, imposed the dualist Orthodox Zoroastrian faith upon his subjects, as the official religion of state. Zoroastrianism was not based upon belief in an omnipotent and just god, but upon a long and enduring struggle between the forces of good and evil. Some historians believe that this religion may have influenced the belief concerning the role of Satan in developing Christianity, and Zoroastrianism certainly influenced the Manichaean, Paulician, and Bogomil heresies, which would impact upon the shores of Asia Minor and the Balkans, at different rates and intensities, between the tenth and the fifteenth centuries, and having indirect influence upon the Albigensians and Paterenes in the Italian Peninsula and France in the late twelfth and early thirteenth centuries.

Unlike Cyrus and Darius, he did not have the same tolerant attitude toward his subjects, and as a result heretics were extirpated throughout the Sasanian empire, with massacres carried out on Jews, Buddhists, Hindus, Manichaens, and Christians.

The Sasanian empire would eventually fall to the Arab-led Islamic invasions that took place between 637 and 651.

"Ormazd, the lord of all things, produced from Infinite Light, a form of fire whose name was that of Ormazd and whose light was that of fire." From Zoroastrian religious text

GUPTA EMPIRE

Tropic of Cancer

India

THE GUPTA EMPIRE, AD 320–480

The Gupta empire united northern India after five centuries of division and political confusion. Founded by a Magadha political figure, probably a wealthy landowner, Chandra Gupta I, a new empire was created by his successors. However, the state never emulated the heavily centralized Mauryan empire. On his accession, Chandra Gupta married a Licchavi princess, thereby gaining high status; the Guptas continued the policy of marrying into other dynasties, the Vakataka family in the Deccan, thereby ensuring friendly relations to the south of their lands. Samudra Gupta succeeded Chandra about 335. According to an inscription on an Asokan pillar at Allahabad, Samudra conquered four kingdoms around Delhi and Uttar Pradesh, neighboring kings to the south and east were forced to pay homage, and campaigns continued through Kalinga to near modern Madras. Nine kings in the western Ganges plain were destroyed; tribal chiefs of central India and the Deccan were coerced into paying tribute, as were the kings of Assam and Bengal and some in Nepal and the Punjab. Old northern tribal republics such as the Yaudheyas resentfully accepted Gupta suzerainty. Furthermore, foreign kings also paid tribute including the Kushan (actually a vassal of the Sasanids), King Meghavanna of Ceylon, and the Shakas. Samudra's son, Chandra Gupta II, acceding to the throne in 379, finally defeated the Shakas and annexed Malura, Gujerat, and Surashtra in western India. Later marriage alliances ensured that the kingdom of Vakataka became virtually part of the Gupta empire, with Chandra's daughter, widow of

the Vakatakan monarch, ruling as regent. Eventually, the Gupta empire succumbed to successive waves of White Hun invasions. Tribute-paying feudatories broke away, and Gupta's power ebbed, the state collapsing into a number of smaller kingdoms about 535.

The Gupta period has been regarded as the classical period of Hindu civilization. The era produced the decimal system of notation, the golden age of Sanskrit and Hindu art, together with contributions to science, medicine, and trade. The empire possessed good roads with adequate pack animals, oxcarts, and elephants. The rivers and port facilities provided other communications. Exports included spices, sandalwood, precious stones, perfume, indigo, and herbs, while imports were made up of

A detail from a Gupta relief showing the Ramayana, *a Sanskrit epic of the adventures of Rama and his wife, Sita.*

Chinese silk, Ethiopian ivory, and Arabian and Bactrian horses to keep the state cavalry bloodlines strong. Indian ships sailed across the Indian Ocean and the Arabian and China Seas, using square-rigged, two-masted vessels. Other departures occurred with Brahmin writers defining social and legal obligations, such as Yanjavalkya admitting documentary evidence. Hindu philosophy developed, and the Yoga sutras taught concentration of mind and body. Literary studies flourished, the most well-known book being the *Kamasutra*. The dramas of Kalidasa, the *Sakuntala* and *Vikramorvasi*, are also famous, the former made known to Europe by its impact on Goethe. Finally, the Gupta period established the preeminent status of the Hindu Brahmin priest, reinforced in Sanskrit literature, and effectively integrating the caste system into the Indian social structure.

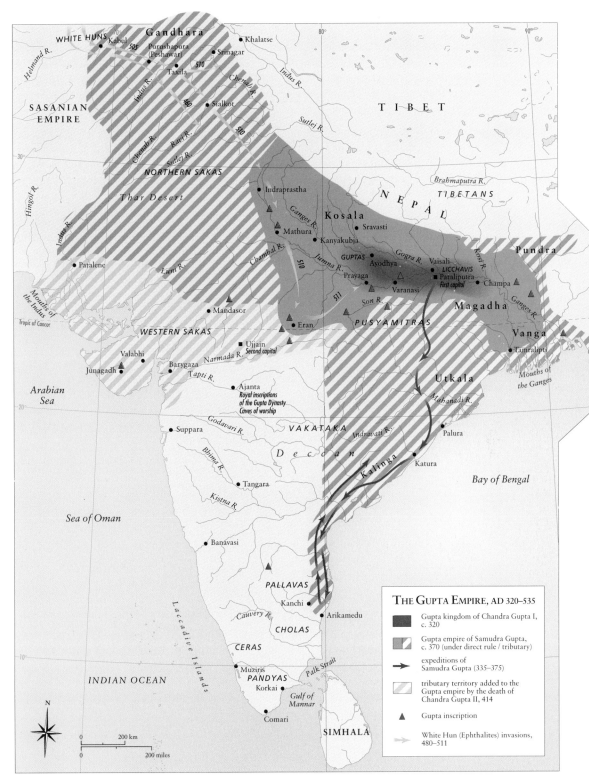

WHITE HUNS · Kabul
Gandhara
· Khalatse
505
Purushapura
(Peshawar)
· Srinagar
Helmand R.
510
Taxila
460
· Sialkot
T I B E T
SASANIAN
EMPIRE
Chenab R.
Indus R.
Indus R.
510
Ravi R.
Chenab R.
Sutlej R.
NORTHERN SAKAS
Sutlej R.
Brahmaputra R.
TIBETANS
· Indraprastha
Thar Desert
N E P A L
Kosala
Pundra
Ganges R.
· Sravasti
· Mathura
· Kanyakubja
Gogra R. Vaisali
· Patalene
Luni R.
Chambal R.
GUPTAS
Ayodhya
LICCHAVIS
Champa
510
Jumna R.
· Prayaga
Pataliputra
First capital
Ganges R.
· Mandasor
511
Varanasi
Magadha
Tropic of Cancer
Eran
Son R.
PUSYAMITRAS
Vanga
WESTERN SAKAS
· Tamralipti
■ Ujjain
Second capital
Mouths of
the Ganges
Valabhi
· Barygaza
Narmada R.
Junagadh
Tapti R.
Utkala
Arabian
Sea
· Ajanta
Royal inscriptions
of the Gupta Dynasty
Caves of worship
Mahanadi R.
· Suppara
Godavari R.
VAKATAKA
Andravati R.
· Palura
D e c c a n
Sea of Oman
Bhima R.
· Tangara
Kalinga
· Katura
Bay of Bengal
Kistna R.
· Banavasi

THE GUPTA EMPIRE, AD 320–535
PALLAVAS
Gupta kingdom of Chandra Gupta I,
c. 320
Cauvery R.
· Kanchi
· Arikamedu
Gupta empire of Samudra Gupta,
c. 370 (under direct rule / tributary)
CHOLAS
CERAS
expeditions of
Samudra Gupta (335–375)
Laccadive Islands
tributary territory added to the
Gupta empire by the death of
Chandra Gupta II, 414
INDIAN OCEAN
· Muziris
PANDYAS
Korkai ·
Gulf of
Mannar
Gupta inscription
· Comari
N
White Hun (Ephthalites) invasions,
480–511
0   200 km
0   200 miles
SIMHALA

55

THE EXPANSION OF PERSIA

Both the Persian Sasanian empire and the Byzantine empire competed for the strategic Caucasian area and aimed to control the desert bordering Syria, Palestine, and Egypt; and throughout the sixth century the Sasanids put constant pressure on Byzantium's eastern frontiers.

Khosroes I (531–579) attacked the Byzantine empire in 540, by conquering Antioch and by seriously menacing Byzantium's eastern frontiers. Plunder from these campaigns against the Byzantines in Syria helped fund his ambitous road- and bridge-building program.

From his capital of Ctesiphon, Khosroes became renowned for the series of reforms that he established, in what would be looked upon as a "golden age,"

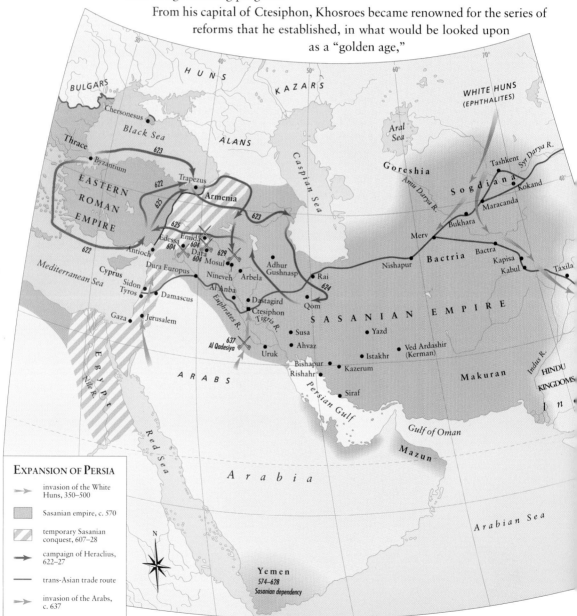

EXPANSION OF PERSIA

→ invasion of the White Huns, 350–500

▨ Sasanian empire, c. 570

▨ temporary Sasanian conquest, 607–28

→ campaign of Heraclius, 622–27

— trans-Asian trade route

→ invasion of the Arabs, c. 637

Yemen
574–628
Sasanian dependency

a period of splendor that would leave a legacy of glory well into the Islamic period that succeeded the Persian Sasanids. Khosroes' tax reforms, probably based upon those introduced to the Roman empire in the fourth century by Emperor Diocletian, resulted in a more stable system for funding the Sasanian state. In the meantime, the civil service was formed, which resulted in a more centralized and more efficient bureaucracy and a strengthening of the monarchy's power. This was enhanced by his reorganization of the army, which extended Persian might at the expense of the Byzantines and their Arab allies in the Syrian desert. Khosroes also fought against the steppe peoples of southern Russia, between the Caucasus and the north-

A detail from a relief of a boar-hunting scene, depicting Khosroes II, who would later be assassinated by his son and successor.

western shores of the Caspian Sea and in Armenia and Lazica. Sasanid armies battled against the Turkmen steppe peoples to the east, and campaigns were led against the nomadic empire of the Hepthalites (White Huns) on the northern border in 568, while in the east the empire spread as far as the Oxus River.

Under his eventual successor, Khosroes II (590–628), the Sasanian empire attained its greatest expansion, with the invasion of Armenia and Mesopotamia. Khosroes took Dara, Emida, and Edessa in 604, sweeping on into central Asia Minor. Damascus was taken in 613 and Jerusalem the following year. In 616, Chalcedon was besieged and fell to the Sasanids.

Eventually this extensive Persian expansion was checked, when the Sasanids were defeated in battle at Issus and Halys, in 622, in a counter offensive by the well-disciplined Byzantine army of Emperor Heraclius. Despite Khosroes' besieging Constantinople, supported by his Avar allies in 626, the Sasanids were eventually routed by the Byzantines, who made major inroads into the heart of Persian territory. Following an indecisive battle at Nineveh, the palace of the "King of Kings" at Dastagird was burned down by the Byzantines, while in 628, internal revolution resulted in the murder of the discredited Khosroes by his ministers.

By 637, the Sasanian state had finally fallen apart after the battle of Al Quadesiya, fought between the Sasanids and the Arabs. By now the Arabs had become the rising power in the Middle East, and both Sasanids and Byzantines had been duped by their Arab rivals.

ARAB CONQUESTS, AD 632–718

The birth and spread of Islam was a
privotal Asian and eventually worldwide event. Islam is predicated
upon Mohammed's prophetic
teachings—the verses of his
revelations being known as
the Koran, commencing in
Mecca (610) when he was
forty. He emphasized
social reform and sought
to replace tribal loyalties
with an Islamic community.
Arousing the enmity of rich conservative merchants, protective of
their local cult, Mohammed fled to
Medina, where he was given supreme
authority to arbitrate local disputes and to
establish Islam. He sought to isolate Mecca by
cutting its trade routes with Syria, and in 630,
the Meccans submitted. Many Arabian tribes converted to Islam, and Mohammed became the most
powerful leader in Arabia, enforced the principles of
Islam, and laid the foundations of an Islamic empire.
During the century after his death (632), Arab armies spread
the Faith through North Africa into Spain and as far east as
Afghanistan and northern India. Later, during the Mughal empire,
Islam was to spread through India and into the Indonesian
Islands. This expansion was based upon the enthusiasm of the
elected caliphs (successors) and the righteousness of the conquerors. Also, the urge for loot and land coincided with the weakness of Byzantium and the Persian empire. Added to this, large-scale
population movements in Arabia saw the eviction of Persian ruling
classes in Bahrain and Oman. Under Caliph Abu Bakr, armies completed the conquest of Arabia and advanced into Iraq and Syria,
where Theodore, the brother of the Byzantine emperor, was defeated at Ajnadain (634). The second caliph, Omar, changed the new
Arabian state into a huge theocratic empire. He invaded Syria, decisively defeated the Byzantines at Yarmuk (636), and took Damascus, Jerusalem, and northern Syria as far as Antioch. A campaign against Persia followed, the Persians
were defeated at Qadisiya (637), Ctesiphon (637), Jalula (637), and finally at
Nehavend (642). An Arab invasion of Egypt in 639 led to another Byzantine
defeat at Heliopolis (640), and the capitulation of Egypt was arranged by
Cyrus, the patriarch of Alexandria (642). Although internecine strife developed
over possession of the caliphate, the policy of expansion continued under the

*Islamic tradition associ-
ates the Dome of the
Rock in Jerusalem with
Mohammed's ascension
on his winged horse into
paradise, although this
has been disputed by
some scholars.*

Omayyids and their successors. In response to Byzantine naval power, the Arabs constructed their own fleet, which saw action at Cyprus and Rhodes. In Asia, Arab power conquered Kabul, Bukhara, and Samarkand, finally acquiring Transoxiana and the Indus region by 711. In North Africa, Carthage was taken by 698, and Tariq crossed the Straits of Gibraltar, defeated the Visigoths (711), and acquired Spain. The final throw in this initial burst of territorial acquisition was a failed attempt to capture the Byzantine capital at Constantinople (718). The Arab conquests resulted in an influx of wealth into Medina, which became a center for Koranic study. The later removal of the capital to Damascus (658), and the restoration of administration and taxation, caused a relative decline of Arabian influence.

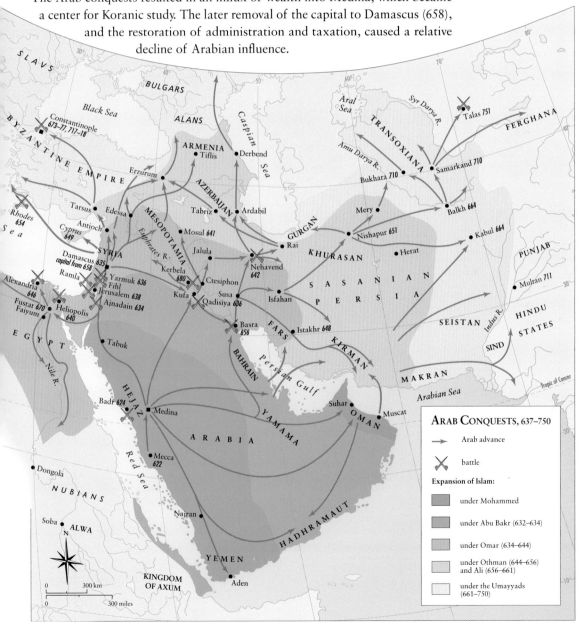

ARAB CONQUESTS, 637–750

→ Arab advance

✕ battle

Expansion of Islam:

- under Mohammed
- under Abu Bakr (632–634)
- under Omar (634–644)
- under Othman (644–656) and Ali (656–661)
- under the Umayyads (661–750)

PART III: PHILOSOPHIES AND EMPIRES

The T'ang period witnessed an artistic and a cultural golden age in China, which reached its heights of achievement in the early eighth century. This was a period in which China was open to external ideas and influences, largely carried by Arabian and Persian seafarers, and merchants using the Silk Road. Significant developments were in music, dance, and painting, with noted painters such as Yen Li-pen, Wu Tao-tzu, and the poet Wang Wei. The greatest achievement was in the field of poetry, with poets such as Li Po, Tu Fu, and Wang Wei, reflecting Taoist and Confucian ideas and beliefs in their works. Some 50,000 works by 2,000 poets have survived, and these have provided historians with a wealth of information on Chinese society. Many of the poets and painters of the period were also administrators in government service, reflecting a balance between public duty and artistic achievement that was true to Confucian and Taoist thinking and education. As a social and political code for the Chinese, Confucianism affected the daily life and culture of Buddhists, Taoists, and Christians alike in China.

Providing an ideal place for the Buddhist idea of meditation, this monastery was built on the "Tiger's Nest" at Takstang in Bhutan.

Neo-Confucianism emerged during the Sung dynasty (960–1279), with the aim of establishing and developing the purity of Chinese tradition at the expense of foreign influences, particularly Buddhist influences introduced from India. Buddhism had come to China in the first century AD and had spread throughout the land between the fall of the Han dynasty in 220 and the rise of the Sung in 960.

Buddhism can be interpreted as a pan-Asian religion and philosophy that, from its roots in northeast India, spread during the sixth century to central and southeast Asia, China, Korea, and Japan. Buddhism has had a tremendous impact upon the spiritual, cultural, and social life of much of the oriental world. Its founder, Siddharta, disturbed by his realization of the inevitability of sickness, old age, and death, had renounced family life as a young man, to become a wandering ascetic, in search of deeper religious understanding and meaning, achieving true enlightenment through meditation. Those who followed him were expected to reach the "middle way," a path between a worldly life and the extremes of self-denial.

Between the second century BC and the second century AD, new Sanskrit/Buddhist texts appeared whose followers called themselves the Mahayana, the followers of the Greater Vehicle. This would become the main version of Buddhism that was to spread throughout East Asia. From the beginning, the human images of Buddha have been an important feature of Buddhism, and this has been reflected in the great number of temples, monasteries, and shrines that have been built throughout Asia.

Although Buddhism and Taoism became prominent in the period that followed the fall of the Han dynasty, Confucianism continued to maintain a hold upon China, and, under the Sui (581–618) and the T'ang (618–907) dynasties, it flourished because of its links with the perceived glories of the Han past. Confucianism would provide the basis of the competitive examinations for government service that became so prominent during the period of these two dynasties. With Confucian thought, linked to government service, the Confucian scholar was expected to spend part of his life working in the civil service, then to withdraw from public life and return to the countryside, where he could develop his private existence. This way of life is reflected in much of the poetry of the T'ang period.

China, in the meantime, achieved the greatest extent of state expansion and imperial conquest; this territorial expansion coincided with the artistic golden age of the T'ang dynasty.

Despite these cultural glories, the political, economic, and social fabric of China was severely rocked by rebellions in the second half of the eighth century that descended into anarchy and warlordism in the late ninth century, so that central authority based upon the Imperial Court was broken, and power shifted to the provinces as the T'ang dynasty collapsed in 907. China fragmented into ten different states that would remain disunited until reunification by the Sung in 979.

By the seventh century, one of the major Asian religions, Buddhism, had spread to Sumatra, reflecting the regular trade links that had developed between India, China, and Sumatra, whereby the Srivijayan kingdom of Sumatra had acted as a regular stopping point for Chinese Buddhist pilgrims going to India.

At the beginning of the seventh century, Japan had fallen under the heavy influence of China; however, Chinese institutions and practices did not always sit well with the Japanese social, economical, and political climate, so progressively, by the beginning of the eighth century, Japan began to move away from Chinese influence, especially in the areas of politics, legal systems, and the arts. This probably explains why the Taika reforms of 702 were necessary and more suited for developing a truly Japanese state. In the cultural field, Chinese influence had

"Heaven holds its place on high and sends down its blessings, hides its form and shows forth its light. Because it holds a high position it is exalted and because it sends down blessings it is benevolent." *Tung Chung-shu*, Confucian philosopher

Hinduism spread from India across southeast Asia to the Indonesian Islands. Above is the Danau Beratan temple in Bali.

been most greatly felt with the impact of the T'ang golden age upon the arts and poetry, but by the eighth century the Japanese were gradually developing their own poetical forms. In the seventh century too, Buddhism had begun to take a hold upon Japanese life, along with Confucianism, although Shintoism, first mentioned in literature toward the end of the sixth century, began to develop as a separate faith and philosophical system, at the heart of which lies the concept of the truthful way of *kami* (meaning "superior," "divine," or "mystical" nature) of the gods and deities.

Although Shinto was heavily influenced by Confucianism, Taoism, and Buddhism, it should nevertheless be recognized as the indigenous religion of Japan. The traditions of Shinto reflect the social life and philosophical beliefs of the Japanese, so that, with the emergence of a unified nation-state, Shintoism became inextricably linked with Japanese political life and government.

Shinto developed in Japan shortly after the introduction of Buddhism in Japan in 538. Yet little is known of its origins. It had no founder, no official sacred scriptures, and no dogma. Nor did it have a tradition of iconic representation before the ninth century, when it became influenced by Buddhist symbols.

Most historians accept that Confucianism was also introduced to Japan in the fifth century AD and that it had become widespread by the seventh century. Confucianism had spread to all those East Asian countries that were influenced by China, most notably Korea, Japan, and Vietnam. Although the way of life had been founded and developed by Confucius during the sixth and fifth centuries BC, it would have a great impact upon Chinese learning, culture, philosophy, and religion for more than two thousand years, and can be interpreted as both a philosophical system and a religion, having become a state cult in the second century BC.

Meanwhile, to the west of China, the Seljuks, a nomadic Turkmen tribe, migrated from central Asia and southeast Russia into the Middle East during the tenth century. They conquered Persia, and established a military sultanate over the Caliphate, by capturing Baghdad. The Seljuk Turks became a serious rival to the Byzantine empire, threatening Byzantium's eastern Anatolian provinces and eventually winning much of Asia Minor. Conflict between the Byzantines and the Seljuks, and the later campaigns of the Crusades, could also from time to time disrupt the flow of goods east and west along the Silk Road, the main trade route linking Byzantium with India and China.

The Seljuk conquest of the Middle East ushered in the beginnings of Turkish power in Asia Minor. Nevertheless, the gradual formation of different factions among the Seljuks, and the internecine strife that ensued, would entail the break up of Seljuk power by 1200, with the exception of Anatolia, where the Seljuks continued to rule until the Mongol Conquest of the thirteenth century.

The Mongols, at the height of their conquests in the twelfth and thirteenth centuries, drew into their sphere of influence China, India, the Near East, Russia, and significant parts of Eastern Europe. Their leader, Genghis Khan, became, at the time of his death in 1227, the greatest conqueror that the world has ever known.

The struggle between Byzantium and the Seljuk Turks also served as a pretext for the launch of the First Crusade, inflicting a series of military expeditions upon Asia; primarily though not exclusively the Crusades centered upon competition for the control of the holy sites between Muslims and Christians, leading to deep enmity between the two faiths between the eleventh and the end of the thirteenth century. There has always been a danger of interpreting the Crusades from a western perspective, concentrating on the achievements of the crusaders, who, as militant pilgrims, conquered the Muslims and freed the Christian holy places. This viewpoint not only glosses over the victories of Saladin at the end of the twelfth century, but also ignores that for the Muslims, the so-called "Crusades" merely formed another front in their many wars with Byzantium and Persia. As such, a stereotypical Westernized and hegemonic mythology of the Crusades has sprung up among many traditional historians, who have interpreted Islam as the enemy of civilization. To some extent this attitude continues to be voiced today, with hostility toward Islam expressed in such often ill-used and misunderstood expressions as "Islamic fundamentalism." The occidental metanarrative often interprets the Europeans as the great educators of the "orientals," bringing them democracy and political freedoms as opposed to the abhorrence of eastern slavery and serfdom. The reality was in fact quite different, since so much cultural, medical, mathematical, and scientific knowledge flowed from East to West, rather than vice versa.

Believed to be Mecca, although some historians have described it to be Medina, this is a fourteenth-century portrayal of the most important site of Islamic pilgrimage.

THE TAIKA REFORM OF JAPAN, 646–710

During the sixth century, the existing Japanese clan system was shaken by Korean immigrants and the import of Chinese civilization, especially the concept of centralization of power in the imperial clan. Conflict between powerful families occurred over the introduction of Buddhism. Against this background, the ruling Soga family were engaged in internecine strife and murder. Empress Suiko (593–628) used crown prince Shotoku to Sinicize forms of government, establish Buddhism, and provide an ideological base for political centralization in the Seventeen-Article "Constitution" (604), a vague conglomeration of Confucian ethics and Chinese political theory. Further interfamily bloodshed led to a coup d'état by the Fujiwara clan, thus giving progressive elements at court the opportunity to implement major reforms.

The Taika reforms were edicts creating general principles of national reorganization. They took many years to implement, and some remained on paper. The main points of the new system were the nationalization of land, but in reality hereditary estates of clan chiefs were returned to them as a salary for official position; the adoption of the Chinese T'ang system of land redistribution and taxation which worked badly; and the reorganization of local and central government. The latter was organized into a council of state controlling eight ministries, themselves divided into departments. This attempt at modern government failed through lack of revenue, itself the result of too many aristocratically owned tax-exempt estates. The Fujiwara clan eventually introduced new civil and penal codes known as the Taika Laws (702), codifying the earlier Taika reforms, attempting to make them suited to the Japanese state. In 710, the imperial capital was shifted from Asuka to Nara. Nara was laid out on the model of Ch'ang-an, the T'ang capital. The following Nara period (710–784) was conspicuous for the flowering of classic Japanese culture.

Poetry and prose were composed in Chinese and

Mount Fujiyama illustrated in this print by Miroshige, served as an emblem of constancy and love of motherland even as Japanese daily life changed form.

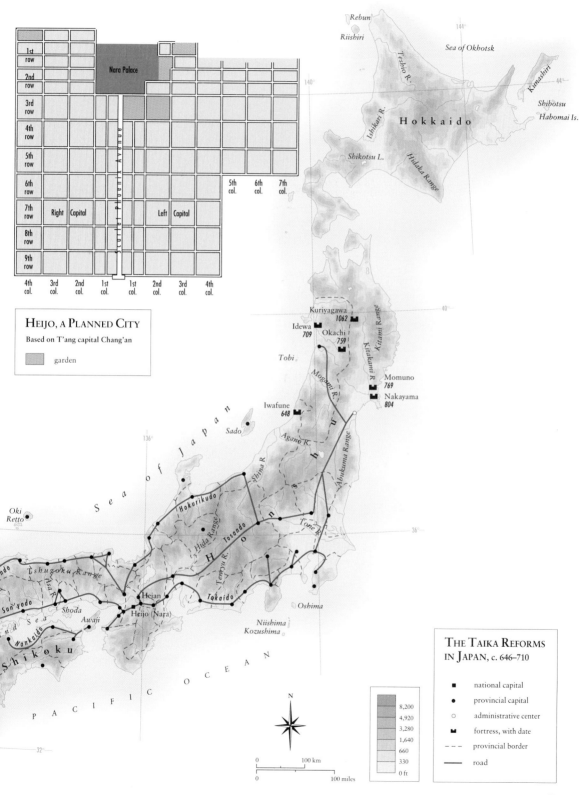

1st row								
2nd row			Nara Palace					
3rd row								
4th row								
5th row								
6th row								
7th row	Right	Capital		Left	Capital			
8th row								
9th row								

5th col.   6th col.   7th col.

4th col. 3rd col. 2nd col. 1st col.   1st col. 2nd col. 3rd col. 4th col.

Scarlet Phoenix Avenue

Heijo, a Planned City

Based on T'ang capital Chang'an

garden

Rebun
Riishiri

Sea of Okhotsk

144°

Teshio R.

Kunashiri

44°

Shibotsu
Habomai Is.

Ishikari R.

Hokkaido

140°

Shikotsu L.

Hidaka Range

40°

Kuriyagawa
1062

Idewa
709

Okachi
759

Kitami Range

Tobi

Kitakami R.

Momuno
769

Nakayama
804

Mogami R.

Iwafune
648

Agano R.

Sado

Abukuma Range

H o n s h u

Shina R.

Oki
Retto

S e a   o f   J a p a n

136°

Hokurikudo

Hida Range

Tosando

Tone R.

36°

H
o
n

Chugoku Range

Tempyu R.

San'indo

Asa R.

Heian

Tokaido

Oshima

San'yodo

Shoda

Heijo (Nara)

Awaji

Niishima
Kozushima

I n l a n d   S e a

Nankaido

S h i k o k u

P A C I F I C   O C E A N

32°

N

The Taika Reforms
in Japan, c. 646–710

- ■ national capital
- ● provincial capital
- ○ administrative center
- ⛫ fortress, with date
- --- provincial border
- — road

	8,200
	4,920
	3,280
	1,640
	660
	330
	0 ft

0   100 km

0   100 miles

Japanese, and the spirit of T'ang China helped produce brilliant examples of art in the fields of architecture, sculpture, and painting. Japanese culture was always adept at incorporating foreign elements deemed appropriate to native art forms. The ceremony consecrating the Great Buddha of the Todai-ji was run by an Indian Brahmin high priest, with music being played by musicians from all over the Far East. In literature, foreign elements can also be found. A compilation of poems in Chinese, the *Kaifuso,* was completed (751), but in 759, the *Manyo-shu* (Anthology of a Myriad Leaves), comprising over 4,000 poems in pure Japanese, was brought together. Only in the next Heian period (794–1185) did a growing independence from Chinese influences develop. The leaders in promoting culture, especially the Buddhist variants, were Emperor Shomu and his consort, Komyo. The Nara period is noticeable for the writing of history. In 712 the *Kojiki,* a history of Japan, was written; in 720, the *Nihonshoki* chronicled the origins of its people, the formation of the Japanese state, and the nature of the national polity. Buddhist fervor is evidenced by the dedication of the Great Buddha (Daibatsu) at Nara. Just before its erection, a Buddhist monk, Gyogi, is alleged to have claimed that Buddhism and Shinto (the original Japanese religion) were two aspects of the same faith wherein Shinto gods were considered to be manifestations of Buddhist deities.

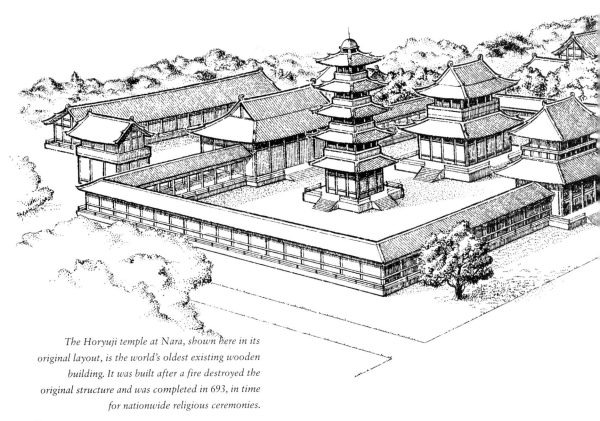

The Horyuji temple at Nara, shown here in its original layout, is the world's oldest existing wooden building. It was built after a fire destroyed the original structure and was completed in 693, in time for nationwide religious ceremonies.

The warrior caste, always an important feature of Japanese life, is exemplified by this fine illustration of Tomoe, a brave woman of the Genji and Heishi period of Japan, c. 900. The warrior caste remained significant until the time of the Meiji Restoration, beginning 1868.

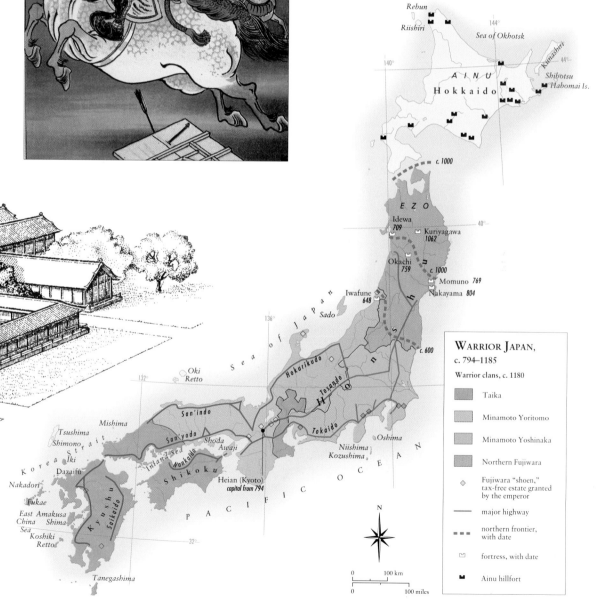

WARRIOR JAPAN,
c. 794–1185

Warrior clans, c. 1180

- Taika
- Minamoto Yoritomo
- Minamoto Yoshinaka
- Northern Fujiwara
- ◇ Fujiwara "shoen," tax-free estate granted by the emperor
- —— major highway
- - - - northern frontier, with date
- ⊡ fortress, with date
- ◼ Ainu hillfort

T'ANG CHINA

In spite of the cultural and artistic golden age of the T'ang dynasty (618–907), in the second half of the ninth century the government had grown gradually weaker in the face of successive rebellions, and the dynasty collapsed in 907.

The T'ang state had been a strong and centralized empire based upon an effective and uniform administrative system. There was a period of internal consolidation throughout the seventh century before the T'ang began to expand abroad into central Asia in the eighth century. However, Chinese expansion and control in central Asia collapsed with the defeat of the T'ang army by the Arabs at Atlach on the Talas River in 751. The situation worsened when, in 755, Lu-shan, a frontier general, began a rebellion by marching on Peking with an army of 150,000 troops and proclaimed himself emperor of a new dynasty, the Yen. The anarchy and unrest lasted until T'ang victory in 763. Immense devastation had been caused throughout China, and despite their victory, T'ang imperial authority

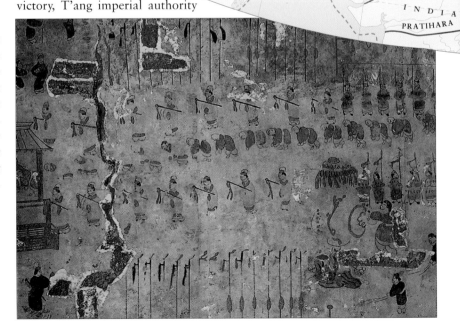

This detail from a fresco was found in an eastern Han tomb. Dating from around AD 140, it shows visiting nomads paying respect to the garrison commander at Nicheng. They are flanked by Chinese soldiers wearing armor and holding spears.

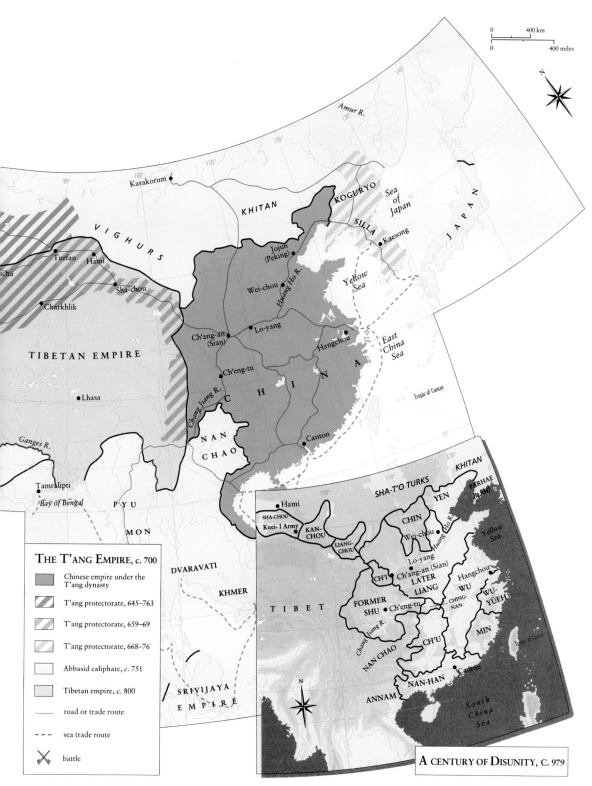

THE T'ANG EMPIRE, c. 700

- Chinese empire under the T'ang dynasty
- T'ang protectorate, 645–763
- T'ang protectorate, 659–69
- T'ang protectorate, 668–76
- Abbasid caliphate, c. 751
- Tibetan empire, c. 800
- —— road or trade route
- – – – sea trade route
- ✕ battle

A CENTURY OF DISUNITY, C. 979

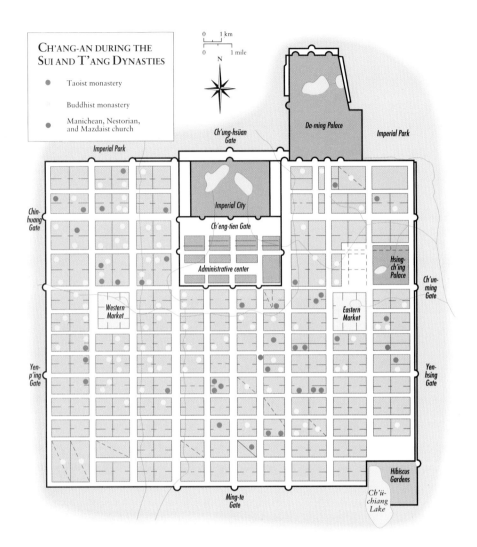

CH'ANG-AN DURING THE
SUI AND T'ANG DYNASTIES

● Taoist monastery

● Buddhist monastery

● Manichean, Nestorian,
and Mazdaist church

0   1 km

0   1 mile

N

Ch'ung-hsüan
Gate

Da-ming Palace

Imperial Park

Imperial Park

Chin-
huang
Gate

Imperial City

Ch'eng-tien Gate

Administrative center

Hsing-
ch'ing
Palace

Ch'un-
ming
Gate

Western
Market

Eastern
Market

Yen-
p'ing
Gate

Yen-
hsing
Gate

Hibiscus
Gardens

Ming-te
Gate

Ch'ü-
chiang
Lake

had been almost destroyed and remained seriously weakened, as the centralized state collapsed and power passed into the provinces. T'ang government would never again be able to assert complete control over the empire.

In the meantime, against the spread and establishment of Islam in Turkestan and the background of internal strife in China, Chinese troops had withdrawn from central Asia, to be replaced by the Uighurs and the Tibetans. One result of the breaking of cultural bonds between China and central Asia was that China became isolated and withdrew in upon itself.

Further rebellions took place, but the situation grew worse in the 870s, with an outbreak of huge peasant unrest throughout China. The roots of the problem lay in growing pressure upon the land following the increase in size of the rural population. This led to economic hardship, which was exacerbated by poor harvests, near-famine, and widespread exploitation by landowners, supported by a harsh bureaucracy. The unrest culminated in the Huang Ch'ao uprising, weakening central authority even further and placing power firmly in the hands of provincial generals. There was constant warfare in northern China and unrest and insecurity elsewhere, leading to further anarchy.

When the T'ang dynasty collapsed in 907, China had split up into ten independent states and would remain divided until reunification under the Sung in 979. Apart from internal fragmentation, China had also lost control of its frontiers, with the threat of the Khitan empire, newly established in Manchuria and Inner Mongolia in the northeast, and the Hsi-Hsia, who had set up a powerful kingdom in the northwest.

A group of nomads from the northern frontier paying homage to the Chinese emperor.

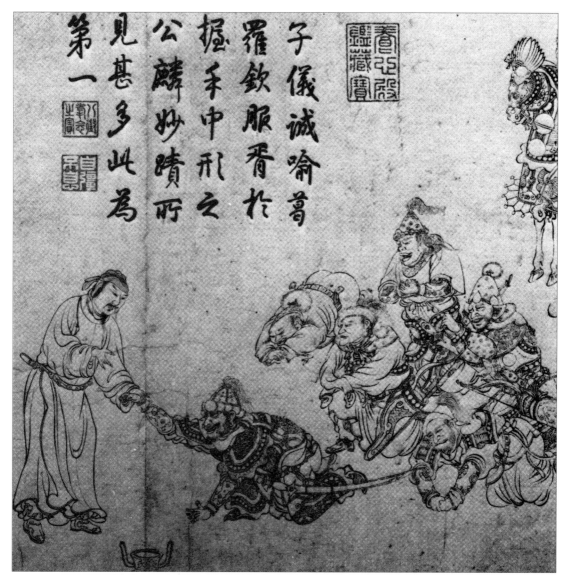

SUNG CHINA

A fine silk painting, displaying the high achievements in pictorial art during the period of the Sung dynasty.

The reunification of China was eventually achieved under the founder of the Sung dynasty, Chao K'uang-yin (960–976) who came to power through a coup d'état in 960. Establishing his capital at Pien, Chao based his political success upon the diplomatic manipulation of potential rivals who would give up their power in exchange for sinecures and titles from the Sung.

In the eleventh century, China arguably had become the world leader in economic development, numeracy, and literacy, and the Sung dynasty witnessed many educational, economic, commercial, and technical developments. Several cities along the southeast coast and its riverine hinterland had populations numbering more than one million. With a growth in commerce and the greater use of credit and paper currency, stimulated by a growth in road networks and canal systems, came the development of a true industrial society, with the mining of coal and iron on a large scale, which in turn stimulated military technology (such as shipbuilding) and printing. The introduction of moveable type to printing assisted the spread of Confucian literature and learning. Against this background, education flourished, with a huge increase in the number of schools to meet the needs of a growing civil service that was recruited through competitive exams.

Chao K'uang-yin had introduced a solid administrative regime through an efficient civil service; however, this declined in its effectiveness during the reign of Chao's successors, who were threatened first by the Lia of the Khitan kingdom, then by the Juchen, Mongolian tribes in the north, who invaded the Sung state. It was Sung China's great wealth and civilization that made it a prey to its barbarian neighbors. In the century of disunity that followed, the Juchen conquered northern China, calling themselves the Chin, but they failed to take Sung territory south of the Yangtze River.

The Chin had been subjects of the Khitans, but with the help of the Sung had broken free to establish their own dynasty, in turn attacking the Sung. Although they employed a Chinese-style administrative system, they continued to employ their own language and alphabet and banned Chinese customs from their army. They were finally destroyed by the Mongols in 1234.

The Sung dynasty later established itself in the South in 1127, under Kao Tsung, who set up his capital at Lin-an (present-day Hangchou). Kao Tsung greatly admired the civil service reforms of his Han predecessors. Despite this the Sung dynasty eventually went into slow decline throughout the twelfth century. The main threat came from the Mongols, led by Ghenghis Khan, who began to make incursions into China with an attack on the northern Chin state in 1211.

SUNG CHINA, c. 1000

SOUTHERN SUNG AND CHIN EMPIRES, 1142

BYZANTIUM AND THE SELJUK TURKS

The Seljuk Turks, originally a nomadic tribe of Oghuz Turkmen that had converted to the Sunni form of Islam, migrated in the tenth century from central Asia and southeast Russia into the Middle East, where they settled in the lands of the Abbasid caliphate. They conquered Persia and imposed a military sultanate over the caliphate, occupying Baghdad in 1055. They then attacked the eastern Anatolian provinces of the Byzantine empire, in eastern and central Asia Minor, in the process, and then turned south against the Fatamids in Egypt.

In 1043, Basil II, Emperor of Byzantium, gained Armenia through tactful diplomacy; however, within a period of twenty years Armenia was in turn conquered by the Seljuk leaders Alp-Arslan and Malik-Shah, along with the annexation of Mesopotamia, Syria, and Palestine. Their conquests led to a series of

BYZANTIUM AND THE SELJUK TURKS

→ major Seljuk campaign

▢ Seljuk Sultinate at its maximum extent, c. 1090

▢ Byzantine empire, c. 1095

▨ territory lost to Byzantine empire and crusaders states, 1097–99

◯ extent of the Khwarizm Shahdom, c. 1220

systematic raids that resulted in the conquest of Asia Minor, which had been so important to the security of the Byzantine empire.

In 1071, the Seljuks defeated the Byzantines at the battle of Manzikert, capturing Emperor Romanus IV Diogenes in the process, and then establishing themselves in Nicea. Threatened on all frontiers, the Byzantine cause was temporarily saved and secured on Byzantium's eastern frontier by the intervention of Emperor Alexius Comnenus, who, on his coronation in April 1081, negotiated with the Seljuks, and diplomatically recognized their claims in Asia Minor, so that he could turn his attentions elsewhere.

This gateway to a Seljuk caravanserai can still be seen in Cappadocia, Turkey.

The Seljuk conquest of the Middle East signified the beginning of Turkish power in that region, and the Seljuks would make a strong impression upon Islam in both a political and a religious sense, as witnessed by the building of mosques and Madrasahs in which religious scholars and state administrators could be educated and trained.

However, despite their impact upon Islam and the Middle East, the Seljuks soon began to quarrel among themselves, and internecine warfare broke out between different factions, largely due to the Seljuk custom of dividing provinces up equally among the male successors of each deceased ruler. By 1200, Seljuk power had been broken, apart from in Anatolia, where they ruled until the Mongol conquest of the thirteenth century.

THE CHRISTIAN CRUSADES

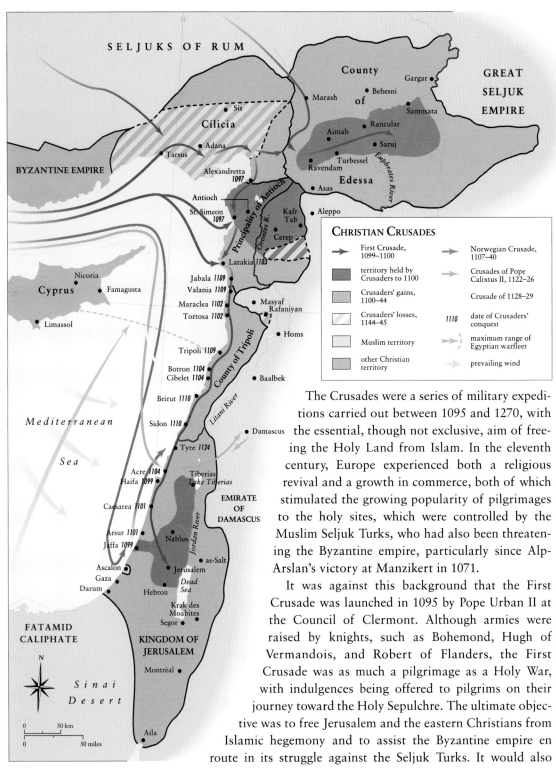

SELJUKS OF RUM

County of Edessa

GREAT SELJUK EMPIRE

Gargar

Marash
Behesni
Samosata
Sis
Rancular
Cilicia
Aintab
Saruj
Adana
Turbessel
Tarsus
Ravendam
Alexandretta *1097*
Asas

BYZANTINE EMPIRE

Antioch
St. Simeon *1097*
Kafr Tab
Aleppo
Cerep

CHRISTIAN CRUSADES

→ First Crusade, 1099–1100	→ Norwegian Crusade, 1107–40
territory held by Crusaders to 1100	→ Crusades of Pope Calixtus II, 1122–26
Crusaders' gains, 1100–44	→ Crusade of 1128–29
Crusaders' losses, 1144–45	*1110* date of Crusaders' conquest
Muslim territory	⇢ maximum range of Egyptian warfleet
other Christian territory	⇒ prevailing wind

Latakia *1103*

Nicoria
Jabala *1109*
Valania *1109*
Cyprus
Famagusta
Maraclea *1102*
Masyaf
Rafaniyan
Tortosa *1102*

Limassol
Homs

Tripoli *1109*

County of Tripoli

Botron *1104*
Cibelet *1104*
Baalbek

Beirut *1110*

Mediterranean
Sidon *1110*

Damascus

Tyre *1124*

Sea
Acre *1104*
Haifa *1099*
Tiberias
Lake Tiberias

EMIRATE OF DAMASCUS

Caesarea *1101*

Arsur *1101*
Jaffa *1099*
Nablus
as-Salt

Ascalon
Gaza
Jerusalem
Darum
Dead Sea
Hebron

Krak des Moabites

FATAMID CALIPHATE
Segor

N
KINGDOM OF JERUSALEM

Sinai Desert
Montréal

0   50 km
0   50 miles

Aila

The Crusades were a series of military expeditions carried out between 1095 and 1270, with the essential, though not exclusive, aim of freeing the Holy Land from Islam. In the eleventh century, Europe experienced both a religious revival and a growth in commerce, both of which stimulated the growing popularity of pilgrimages to the holy sites, which were controlled by the Muslim Seljuk Turks, who had also been threatening the Byzantine empire, particularly since Alp-Arslan's victory at Manzikert in 1071.

It was against this background that the First Crusade was launched in 1095 by Pope Urban II at the Council of Clermont. Although armies were raised by knights, such as Bohemond, Hugh of Vermandois, and Robert of Flanders, the First Crusade was as much a pilgrimage as a Holy War, with indulgences being offered to pilgrims on their journey toward the Holy Sepulchre. The ultimate objective was to free Jerusalem and the eastern Christians from Islamic hegemony and to assist the Byzantine empire en route in its struggle against the Seljuk Turks. It would also allow the land-hungry younger sons of the European nobility, who had been excluded from feudal inheritance by the system of primogeniture, to gain lands in the East, a process that was enhanced by the Norman conquest of Sicily. In the First Crusade, excesses, particularly against the Jews, were committed by European armies, swelled by the popular enthusiasm of huge crowds of pilgrims and the political ambitions of barons, as they marched through central and eastern Europe. Many would be ambushed and massacred by the Turks on their arrival in Asia Minor.

Antioch was taken by Bohemond in 1098 after a siege lasting many months, and Jerusalem fell to the Crusaders in July 1099; its Muslim and Jewish inhabitants were put to the sword.

The Latin kingdom of Jerusalem was founded by Baudoin in 1100, alongside a loose federation made up of the Principality of Antioch, and the counties of Edessa and Tripoli. These were defended by a line of "Crusader" castles along the Palestinian littoral.

The fall of Edessa to the Turks in 1144 resulted in the Second Crusade, led by Louis VII, King of France, and the Emperor Conrad III. When their forces, numbering 50,000, arrived in Syria, instead of retaking Edessa, they laid siege to Damascus in 1148, but failed to take it, and with the ensuing defeat, accusations flew in all directions, bringing to a low ebb relations between Europe and the Crusader states.

Saladin, the Muslim sultan of Egypt, Syria, Yemen, and Palestine, was the founder of the Ayyubid dynasty. In 1169, at the age of thirty-one, he had been appointed both commander of the Syrian forces and vizier of Egypt. Later he used his wealthy agricultural possessions in Egypt to finance his control of Syria, which he controlled with a small but well-disciplined army. Between 1174 and 1186, all the Muslim territories of Syria, northern Mesopotamia, Palestine, and Egypt were under his control.

Unlike the internecine rivalry of previous Muslim leaders, which had hindered their resistance to the Christian Crusaders, Saladin was a determined and virtuous ruler who gained a reputation for firmess and fairness and propagated the concept of Jihad (holy war)—the Muslim equivalent of the Christian Crusade.

In 1187 Saladin destroyed a Crusader army at Hattin, near Tiberias in northern Palestine, and then overran most of the Kingdom of Jerusalem. Within three months, Acre, Toron, Beirut, Sidon, Nazareth, Caesarea, Nablus, Jaffa, and Ascalon had fallen to the Muslim armies, and at the beginning of October 1187, Jerusalem, holy city to both Christian and Muslim alike, fell to Saladin after eighty-eight years in Frankish hands.

Unlike the earlier Christian conquest of Jerusalem, which had been marked by its ruthless barbarity, the Holy City was occupied by Muslim troops in a more civilized fashion. The cause of the Crusaders had been dealt a serious blow, and they now only controlled three cities on the Levantine coast, of which Tyre became the rallying point of the Christian cause.

> "Then the Muslims returned to the attack against the Franks and they went back up the hill. When I saw them retreating with the Muslims in pursuit, I cried out in joy, 'We have beaten them.' My father turned to me and said: 'Be silent. We shall not defeat them until that (red) tent of the king falls.' As he spoke, the tent fell."
> Saladin's son al-Afdal 'Ali, at the Battle of Hattin

SUMATRA AND THE SRIVIJAYA KINGDOM

Toward the end of the seventh century, Srivijaya became the dominant kingdom of Sumatra and built up a trading empire that eventually controlled and influenced the Straits of Malacca and Sunda, all of Sumatra, the western half of Java, the Malay Peninsula, especially control of the isthmus of Kra, and parts of Borneo. Its authority was recognized as far away as Ceylon and southern China. Arab and Chinese sources show the importance of the kingdom. Rulers at Srivijaya's capital, Palembang, were determined to control all the region's harbors in order to compete in and monopolize the China trade. China relied on foreign shipping for its imports, especially from

EMPIRE
• Ava
▲ ■ Pagan
OF PAGAN
THAI
Pegu •
MONS
Sukhothai •
DVARAVATI MONS
KHMER EMPIRE
• Ayuthia
■ Angkor
Andaman Is.

Andaman

Sea

° Nicobar Is.

DAI-VIET
• Thang-Long
(Hanoi)
T'ANG CHINA
Hainan

CHAMPA
▲ Vijaya (Binh Dinh)
▲ Panduranga

Gulf of Siam

Luzon

South China Sea

PACIFIC OCEAN

Mindanao

Sulu Sea

Celebes Sea

Brunei •
DUNSUN

Ackin •
Atjeh • Perlak
S u m a t r a
Strait of Malacca
• Malacca
• Tumasik
(Singapore)
▲ Muaro
▲ Takas
Pandang Lawas ▲
KINGDOM OF SRIVIJAYA

Malay Peninsula

Santabong •
DYAKS
B o r n e o
Makakam •
NGASU
Celebes
• Luwu
BUGIS

INDIAN OCEAN

Malayu •▲
(Jambi)
Srivijaya ■▲
(Palembang)

Java Sea

Macassar •

N

Flores
Timor

Borobudur
▲ Singhasari
Madjapahit ▲
Prambanan
J a v a
Bali
Sumbawa

SOUTH EAST ASIA AND THE SRIVIJAYA KINGDOM, c. 1200

- - -   furthest extent of T'ang China

→   Thai peoples moving south

▲   Hindu/Buddhist temple, 600–1300

India, and Srivijaya became a transit point for this seaborne trade. It would be incorrect to see Srivijayan power as political control of its "empire." Warships were needed to patrol the seas, and many islands and their rulers identified with Srivijayan interests and refrained from piracy and cooperated in controlling would-be competitors in northern Sumatra. Thus, Srivijayan rulers had to provide wealth and career opportunities to its allies to prevent this fragmented geographical region from falling out of their orbit. The empire was also subject to attack. In 1025, Rajendracola Deva I of the Indian Cholas raided Srivijaya, crippling it in the short term and certainly reducing its power in the longer term. While the entrepôt trade flourished, Srivijayan power continued, but when Chinese ships began long sea voyages and accessed different areas of production and resources in the Indonesian archipelago, then Srivijayan power and influence declined. Increased piracy in the Sunda and Malacca Straits furthered weakness when traders sought alternative and safer routes. This deterioration was compounded by the consolidation of petty Javanese states, which led to the rise of Singhasari in eastern Java. Its maharajah, Kertanagara, a beneficiary of reoriented Chinese trade, challenged Srivijaya and destroyed its influence, but remained an heir to its aims and pretensions.

The temple group at Panataram in eastern Java, built around 1370, is a fine example of Hindu culture. The style has now become almost entirely Javanese.

The Chinese Buddhist I-Ching mentions Srivijaya in his writings; he thought Palembang a suitable site to study Buddhist texts because it possessed more than a thousand learned monks. Inscriptions at Palembang show that the Tantric school of Mahayana Buddhism arrived in Palembang in the seventh century, shortly after its rise in India. This phenomenon points to the regular and swift shipping contacts between India and Sumatra. Srivijaya became a stopping point for Chinese Buddhist pilgrims going to India, and Srivijayan rulers even founded monasteries at Negapatam in India. Archaeological excavations near Palembang have revealed large quantities of Buddhist relics and statuary from the Musi River.

Srivijaya was just one of a series of southeast Asian kingdoms: Pagan in Burma, Angkor in Cambodia, and Thailand's Champa kingdom. Major temple complexes were built, noticeably in the Khmer kingdom of Angkor. Eventually, these kingdoms succumbed to outside attacks. Pagan was destroyed by Mongols and then the Shans, while Angkor was ravaged by the new Thai power of the Sukhothai kingdom; Champa fell to the Dai Viet, ending the "classical" period of southeast Asian history.

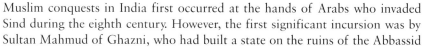

MUSLIM EMPIRE IN INDIA, C. 1175

The tomb of the renowned builder Sultan Tughlug.

Muslim conquests in India first occurred at the hands of Arabs who invaded Sind during the eighth century. However, the first significant incursion was by Sultan Mahmud of Ghazni, who had built a state on the ruins of the Abbassid realm. He raided India over twenty times between 1000 and 1027, during which he annexed the Punjab. In 1160, the Gaznivids were ousted from Ghazni by Muhammed of Ghur. Beginning his campaigns in India in 1175, he conquered Hindustan by capturing Multan and Uch. In 1186, he destroyed the Ghaznavid empire and defeated the Hindu Rajputs at the battle of Tararori near Delhi. Muslim tactics and campaigns were based upon mobile cavalry. The use of military adventurers from central Asia, a good logistical organization, and constant success bred further recruits.

Advances were made into Delhi (1193), Bihar (1197), Bengal (1199), and the Chandella state of Bundelkhand (modern Madhya Pradesh). By 1205, the Ghurids had conquered the Indo-Ganges plain. When Muhammed died, his viceroy in Delhi, the Turkestan slave Qutb-ud-Din Aybak, proclaimed himself Sultan of Delhi, founding the Slave Dynasty. The following major Muslim ruler, Ala-ud-din (1296–1316), consolidated the empire by ravaging Gujerat, seizing Malwa (1305) and the Deccan (1313). Ala-ud-din introduced taxation based upon acreage, using the revenue to finance his military exploits. Price and wage controls helped prevent inflation when his army with all its followers and men and money arrived in a region. The army numbering nearly 500,000 men, big enough to defeat two Mongol invasions (1304 and 1306) and to extort tribute and recognition from Hindu kings. Ala-ud-din married into an important Hindu family, this event being part of an attempt to establish Muslim-Hindu participation in rule.

Despite harsh taxation, a textile industry developed, and international trade grew with the west, especially with Egypt. The last significant sultan was Muhammed Tuhgluq (1325–1351). He destroyed Buddhist monasteries and texts, and a special tax (jizya) was levied on Hindus. His attempts to conquer southern India failed, and his harsh treatment of the population, Muslim and Hindu alike, led to a series of rebellions. A Muslim governor seceded and founded the sultanate of Madwa, while various Hindu rebellions resulted in the creation of the important state of Vijayanagar, which became the focus of resistance to Islam.

The disorder that was the sultanate of Delhi was in no position to face the invasion of Tamerlane (Timur) in 1398. Tamerlane's pretext was that the Delhi sultanate was too tolerant of Hinduism. In a brilliant four-month campaign, bypassing disunited Muslim and Hindu forces or allowing them to submit, he reached Delhi and defeated the sultan at Panipat. Slaughtering some 50,000 Hindu captives, Tamerlane then attacked and sacked Delhi and retired to Samarkand after annexing the Punjab. Thereafter, the sultanate became merely one of several northern Indian states amid new Rajput and Muslim political units.

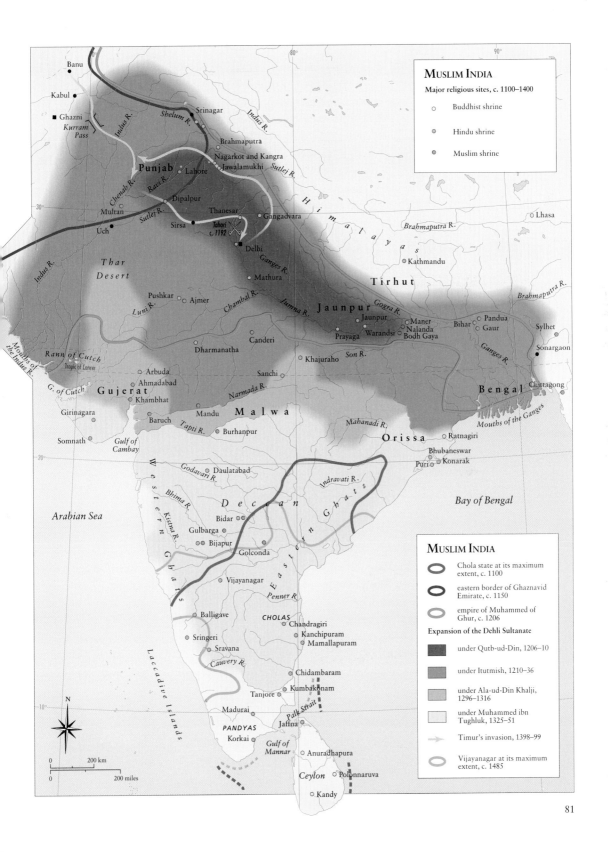

MUSLIM INDIA

Major religious sites, c. 1100–1400

○ Buddhist shrine

○ Hindu shrine

○ Muslim shrine

MUSLIM INDIA

⬭ Chola state at its maximum extent, c. 1100

⬭ eastern border of Ghaznavid Emirate, c. 1150

⬭ empire of Muhammed of Ghur, c. 1206

Expansion of the Dehli Sultanate

■ under Qutb-ud-Din, 1206–10

■ under Itutmish, 1210–36

■ under Ala-ud-Din Khalji, 1296–1316

□ under Muhammed ibn Tughluk, 1325–51

→ Timur's invasion, 1398–99

⬭ Vijayanagar at its maximum extent, c. 1485

THE EMPIRE OF ANGKOR, C. 1180

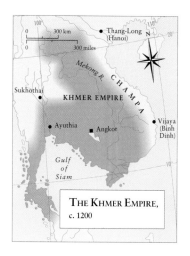

THE KHMER EMPIRE, c. 1200

The Angkor empire lasted from 802 to 1431, when this Khmer civilization was finally overwhelmed by Thai attacks. The capital city, Angkor, is noted for its superb architecture, especially the temple known as Angkor Wat, the most famous of one thousand temples crowded into 120 square miles. The Cambodian kingdom was created by Jayavarman II, who established the ruler as a god-king and chose the Great Lake region as the focus of his power. The surrounding areas included a network of reservoirs and canals controlling the water supply for rice farming. A later ruler, Yasovarman I (889–900), continued the development of the irrigation system and accumulated power, which, exploited by future rulers, led to the subjugation of large parts of contemporary Thailand, the Malaysian Peninsula, and the Chams. The Khmer monarchs consistently built increasingly complex temples dedicated to Hindu gods. Angkor Wat, built by Suryavarman II (1113–1150), sanctified him as the incarnation of Vishnu, the Hindu preserver and savior. The temple comprises a huge rectangle containing concentric walled courtyards surrounding five lotus-shaped towers, showing a blend of Hindu and Buddhist culture.

Jayavarman VII (1181–1219) was a most distinguished and able king, noted for building many temples. Even though the Chams devastated his capital in 1177, he managed to drive them out, and he constructed the Angkor Thom complex containing the Bayon temple, which inaugurated Mahayana Buddhism in Cambodia. He then succeeded in pushing his borders to the coast of Vietnam (acquiring Champa) to Pagan in Burma and into Laos. After Jayavarman's death, internal revolts and foreign attacks led Angkor to decline. Excessive tax demands and neglect of the irrigation system caused rebellions, while the population also suffered epidemics of malaria and visitations of the plague.

Another factor possibly stimulating change and dissent was the introduction of Therevada Buddhism which did not require great temples as did Hinduism and Mahayana Buddhism. Additionally, the Therevada variant undermined the rigid social order, generating unrest. This new ideology resulted in the loss of carved Sanskrit temple inscriptions, thus decreasing historical evidence and clouding the shape of later events. Angkor was further weakened by the growth of several kingdoms in southeast Asia.

In Burma, various Mon and Burmese peoples were establishing states and becoming rivals; the Sumatran Srivijaya empire and the Javanese Sailendras dynasty were also potential threats. Most dangerous were the Thais, who founded the state of Sukhothai in 1238. Several attacks were mounted on Angkor, resulting in brief periods of occupation, and the Khmers were eventually forced to abandon Angkor in favor of other capitals. As Khmer control weakened, vassal states assumed independence and became autonomous. Angkor Wat and Angkor Thom were quietly surrendered to the encroaching jungle.

Angkor Wat, part of Angkor, the capital of the Khmer empire, located in the alluvial flood plain north of the lake Tonle Sap.

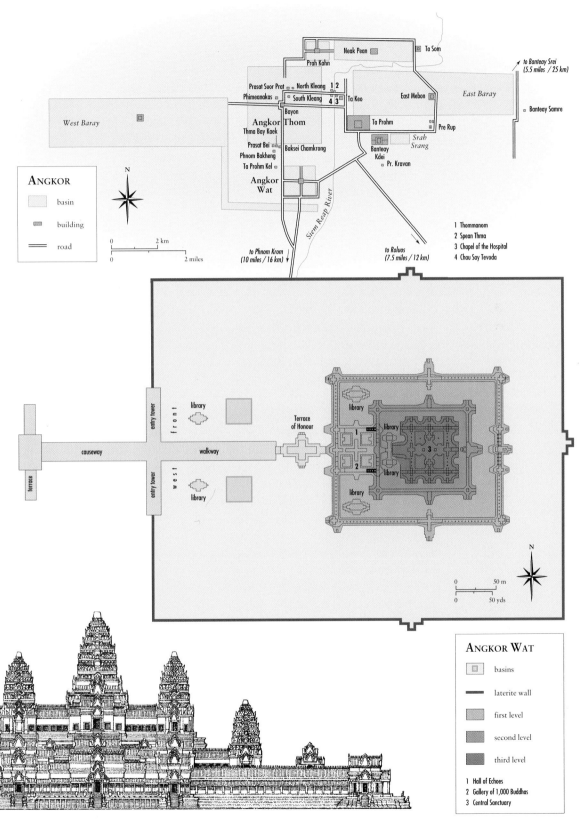

ANGKOR

basin

building

road

N

0   2 km

0   2 miles

West Baray

Neak Pean   Ta Som

Prah Kahn

to Banteay Srei
(5.5 miles / 25 km)

Prasat Suor Prat   North Kleang   1 2

Phimeanakas   South Kleang   4 3   Ta Keo   East Mebon   East Baray

Bayon

Angkor Thom   Ta Prohm   Pre Rup

Banteay Samre

Thma Bay Kaek

Prasat Bei   Baksei Chamkrong   Srah Srang

Phnom Bakheng   Banteay Kdei

Ta Prohm Kel   Pr. Kravan

Angkor Wat

Siem Reap River

to Phnom Krom
(10 miles / 16 km)

to Roluos
(7.5 miles / 12 km)

1 Thommanom
2 Spean Thma
3 Chapel of the Hospital
4 Chau Say Tevoda

terrace

causeway

entry tower

front

library

Terrace of Honour

walkway

west

entry tower

library

library

library

1   library

2   library

library

library

3

N

0   50 m

0   50 yds

ANGKOR WAT

basins

laterite wall

first level

second level

third level

1 Hall of Echoes
2 Gallery of 1,000 Buddhas
3 Central Sanctuary

MONGOL CONQUESTS

Ghenghis Khan in state surrounded by his attendants. The luxury of his court almost contradicts the fact that the Great Khan remained a nomad to the end of his life.

"Happiness lies in conquering one's enemies, in driving them in front of oneself, in taking their property, in savouring their despair."
Ghenghis Khan (c. 1167–1227)

The Mongol history makes nonsense of chronological and territorial divisions. In an astonishingly short time this nomadic people drew into their orbit China, India, the Near East, and Europe and left ineffaceable marks behind them. Yet there is no physical focus for their history except the felt tents of their ruler's encampment; they blew up like a hurricane to terrify half a dozen civilizations, slaughtered and destroyed on a scale the twentieth century alone has emulated, and then disappeared almost as suddenly as they came. They demand to be considered alone as the last and most terrible of the nomadic conquerors.

A group of peoples speaking a language of the Mongol family, who had long lived on the remote arid grasslands in the cold heart of Asia, occasionally raided their neighbors. Generally, China played off one tribe against another in the interests of its own security. Two tribes among them, the Tatars and those who became known as the Mongols, competed, and on the whole the Tatars had the best of it. They drove one young Mongol to extremes of bitterness and self-assertion. The date of his birth is uncertain, but in the 1190s he became khan to his people. A few years later he was supreme among the Mongol tribes and was acknowledged as such by being given the title of Chenghis Khan. By an Arabic corruption of this name, he was to become known in Europe as Ghenghis Khan. He extended his power over other peoples in central Asia, and in 1215 defeated (though he did not overthrow) the Chin state in northern China and Manchuria. This was only the beginning. By the time of his death, in 1227, he had become the greatest conqueror the world has ever known.

He seems unlike all earlier nomad warlords. Ghenghis genuinely believed he had a mission to conquer the world. Conquest, not booty or settlement, was his aim, and what he conquered he often set about organizing in a systematic way. This led to a structure that deserves the name "empire" more than do most of the nomadic polities. He was superstituous, tolerant of religions other than his own paganism, and, said a Persian historian, "used to hold in esteem beloved and respected sages and hermits of every tribe, considering this a procedure to please God." Indeed, he seems to have held that he himself was the recipient of a divine mission. This religious eclecticism was of the first importance, as was the fact that he and his followers (except for some Turks who joined them) were not Muslim, as the Seljuks had been when they arrived in the Near East. Not only was this a matter of moment to Christians and Buddhists—there were both Nestorians and Buddhists among the Mongols who did not identify with the religion of the majority in the Near East.

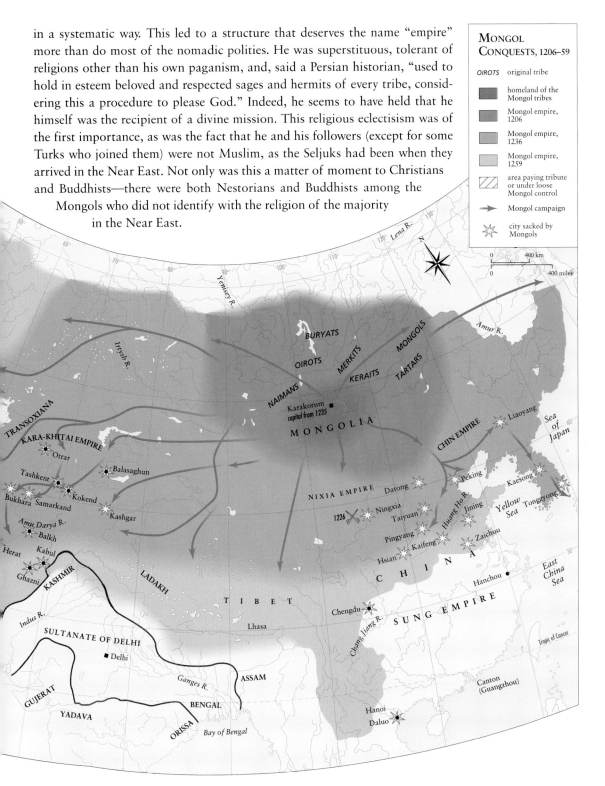

MONGOL CONQUESTS, 1206–59

OIROTS   original tribe

homeland of the Mongol tribes

Mongol empire, 1206

Mongol empire, 1236

Mongol empire, 1259

area paying tribute or under loose Mongol control

Mongol campaign

city sacked by Mongols

THE EMPIRE OF THE GREAT KHAN

The conquest of China, begun by Ghenghis Khan, was finally achieved by his grandson, Kublai Khan (1215–1294), who founded the Yüan dynasty. Kublai Khan became ruler of the vaste swath of Mongol territories and possessions that included the II Khan empire in Persia, the empire of Chagatai, the empire of the Golden Horde, and the steppes.

With the help of his brother, Monge, Kublai Khan took southern China and invaded Tibet, Annam, and Tonkin between 1250 and 1259. He then turned his attention to northern China, forcing the Kin Tatars out of the region between 1260 and 1279.

Kublai Khan's capital, Chanbalik, was built on the present-day site of Beijing, which became the power base of the Yüan dynasty (1279–1368) and replaced the Sung after eight years of conflict .

To govern China, Kublai Khan adapted to a Chinese style of rule, turning against the traditional nomadic life of the Mongols. He placed a heavy reliance upon Chinese civil servants, alienating many Mongols.

Under Kublai Khan, Buddhism became the state religion. Although he tolerated other religions (as had Ghenghis Khan before him), favoritism toward Buddhism fluorished, especially enhancing the importance of Tibetan lamas, and led to strong Chinese resentment. Despite such tensions, Kublai Khan succeeded in reunifying China, which had been divided since the end of the T'ang dynasty.

Kublai Khan engaged in a series of successful colonial wars against Burma and Korea. However, in a further series of expensive wars, he met setbacks and disastrous defeats with his invasions of Japan and Java. This became especially acute in his attempted seaborne invasions of Japan in 1274 and 1281, when his landing forces were practically wiped out.

Improved communications and the security of trade routes under Mongol control made travel between Europe and Asia more accessible. Even so, it was only the privileged foreign merchants, such as the Venetian traveler Marco Polo, who really benefited from their contact with Yüan China. Such disparities led to even greater resentment among the indigenous population.

At the end of the day the Yüan dynasty was disliked by its Chinese citizens, who resented the Mongol ruling class along with its non-Chinese supporters. The crisis was exacerbated by the ineptitude of Kublai Khan's successors. Increasing inflation and civil wars with rival Mongol rulers in the steppes finally led to revolt.

The Yüan dynasty was overthrown by Chu Yüan Chang, who established the Ming dynasty as the Mongols withdrew once again to the steppes.

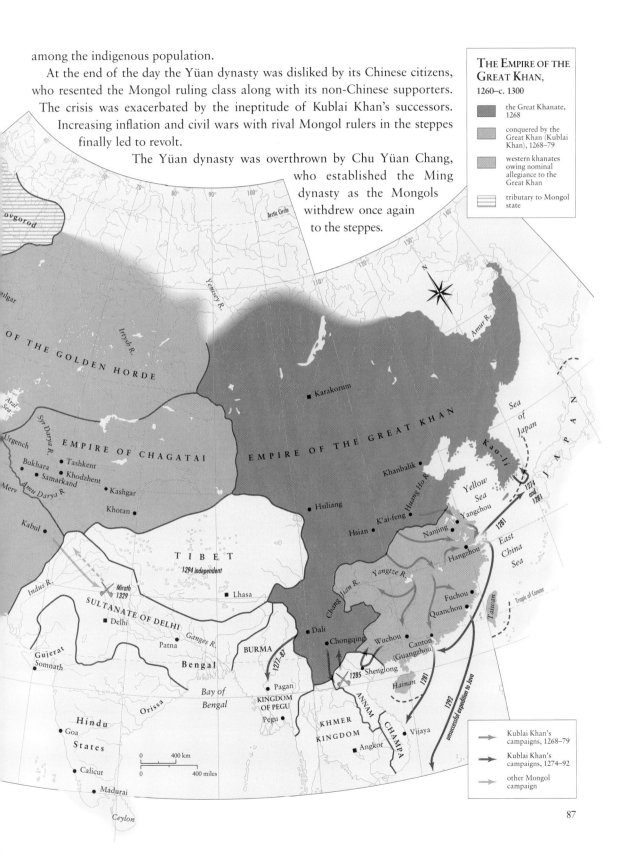

THE EMPIRE OF THE GREAT KHAN, 1260–c. 1300

- the Great Khanate, 1268
- conquered by the Great Khan (Kublai Khan), 1268–79
- western khanates owing nominal allegiance to the Great Khan
- tributary to Mongol state

→ Kublai Khan's campaigns, 1268–79
→ Kublai Khan's campaigns, 1274–92
→ other Mongol campaign

PART IV: CONQUEST, CONSOLIDATION, AND DECLINE

The Ottomans rose to power in the thirteenth century, largely due to the weakness of neighboring empires. Between 1300 and 1481, the Ottomans expanded their power continuously, either through conquest, as demonstrated by their incursions into the Balkans, or through the purchase of territory, especially from Byzantium. This meant that by the beginning of the fifteenth century not only had the whole of Anatolia fallen under Ottoman rule, but the Ottoman Turks had also made deep incursions into Thrace and Macedonia, winning vast tracts of Byzantine, Serbian, and Bulgarian territory. Later, in the sixteenth century, the Ottomans conquered most of Hungary, following the battle of Mohacs (1526), eventually putting pressure upon the Holy Roman empire and even treating Poland as a dependency. In 1575, the Turks invaded Austria from Bosnia and had begun to threaten Muscovy in the northeast, laying siege to Astrakhan in 1569, and advancing on the Don River. By 1571, led by the Khan of Crimea, Ottoman ships crossed the Oka River and burned Moscow. They took some

Tomb of Osman I, founder of an empire that would eventually stretch from Morocco to the Caspian and from Vienna to Nubia.

100,000 prisoners, who were sold into slavery.

The Ottomans also increased their hold on the eastern Mediterranean. They captured Chios in 1566, took Naxos in 1567 and Cyprus in 1570, only to suffer a setback at the battle of Lepanto in 1571, when the Turkish fleet was defeated by an alliance of Spain, Genoa, and Venice, led by Don Juan of Austria.

Despite this period of conquest and expansion, decline gradually set in after the reign of Suleiman I "The Magnificent" (1520–1566), due to widespread administrative weakness and corruption and the poor quality of successive sultans, such as: Selim the Sot (1566–1574); Murad III (1574–1595), and Mehemed IV (1595–1603). Occasionally these despots engaged themselves in excessive acts of cruelty. Murad III had his brothers executed, on his accession to the throne, fearing that they might become potential rivals. Later, on his deathbed, Murad had nineteen of his sons strangled in the interest of the succession of his eldest son.

In the meantime, Ottoman control of maritime trade routes gradually slipped out of Turkish hands and into the hands of Greek merchants and seamen, who would eventually build up an almost total monopoly of the Ottoman empire's internal and external trade.

The decay of empire was not helped by the weakness of successive sultans, who were constantly frustrated by the rise to power of the *devsirme* class of young Christian males, who mostly came from the Balkans. As children, they were taken from their homes and transported to Constantinople, where they were converted to Islam, to spend the rest of their lives serving the Ottoman state as personal slaves to the sultan. An excellent narrative account of this process may be found in Ivo Adric's historical novel about Bosnia, *Bridge over the Drina*. The *devsirme* not only provided able administrators, but also a military caste known as the Janissaries. With the passing of time, the *devsirme* gradually became a ruling class that could confront the power of the sultan. Although there were reforms in the seventeenth century, these failed to arrest the decline. In the meantime, the rise of powerful nation-states in Europe, concomitant with the creation of an alliance system against the Turks, ensured that the Ottomans would gradually be driven from Europe. The process of Ottoman decline accelerated in the eighteenth century, and although the Ottoman empire still sprawled over eastern Europe, Asia Minor, and North Africa, it was no longer considered by its neighbors to be a serious threat. What the Ottomans needed to maintain their power was centralization, and this was not in evidence, as the situation was exacerbated by court intrigues in Constantinople, the meddling of the Janissaries, and the general laziness of the sultans. The imperial finances fell into a state of anarchy, with tax gathering being farmed out to a host of middlemen, who took as much as they could, involving themselves in widespread corruption.

Successive sultans became dependent upon the Orthodox Christian Greeks to govern the Christian Slav principalities, which weakened their overall control even further; and against a background of terror and cruelty in the treat-

The great period of the Ottoman expansion occurred during the reign of Suleiman I "The Magnificent," even leading to an Ottoman fleet attack on the French town of Toulon in 1545.

ment of local populations by the grand vizirs, seething resentment became widespread among the subject peoples of the Ottoman empire throughout the Balkans. By the beginning of the nineteenth century, the Balkan peoples would begin to openly oppose the Ottoman state.

In the meantime, China had been open to the ravages of Mongol incursions throughout the fourteenth century, although the rise to power in the late 1360s of a new dynasty, the Ming, would reverse these trends. The Ming reformed the army and stimulated the Chinese economy and trade, so that throughout the sixteenth century, industry would flourish in the great cities of the Yangtze Delta. Harnessed to this growth in commerce and trade came the consolidation of power within China and the gradual expansion of power, so that China dominated Korea, Mongolia, and Turkestan at the beginning of the fourteenth century and made inroads into Vietnam and Burma.

Despite this aggressive foreign policy, by the sixteenth century, the Ming empire was in a gradual state of decline. With a high birthrate, China could no longer feed its sixty million inhabitants, even though the Chinese had begun to cultivate maize, which had been introduced from the Persian Gulf. There were court intrigues, corrupt officials, exploitation by feudal landlords, and minor disturbances in the provinces, but the real problems came from outside.

By the second half of the sixteenth century, ocean voyages were proscribed; a weakened Ming empire was no longer able to defend its frontiers or fight off incursions by Malay and Japanese pirates, or halt the invasion of Yunnan by Burmese warriors. Meanwhile, Portuguese merchants had established a trading post at Macao between 1514 and 1552, although this was surrounded by a barrier blocking contact with the interior of China. The Ming authorities had begun to discourage communications with the outside world in the early fourteenth century, but by the sixteenth century, China began to withdraw more and more in upon itself against the growing threat of Mongol pressure from the North and Japanese invasions from the sea.

When the Ming were overthrown in 1644, the Manchu dynasty (1644–1912) came to power in China. This would be the last of the Chinese imperial dynasties. At the height of their power, at the end of the seventeenth century, the Manchu would witness an enormous extension of Chinese territory, with the empire tripling in size. From Mukden (present-day Shenyang) they invaded Korea in 1637, while Inner Mongolia became a dependency between 1629 and 1635. Formosa (Taiwan) was occupied in 1683, and the Chakhars of Outer Mongolia were defeated in 1676 and forced to recognize Manchu sovereignty. In the meantime, the Manchu had checked Russian expansion on the Amur River by 1682. By the beginning of the eighteenth century, Mongolia, Dzungaria, the Tarim basin, the area to the east of Lake Balkhash, and Tibet were under Chinese control. The Manchu carried out four attacks against Burma between 1788 and 1792; they launched an expedition into Nepal and invaded Tonking in 1788 and 1792. Nevertheless, it can be argued that Manchu expansion had been partly motivated by a fear of Russian expansion into Siberia and the presence of the British and French in India and Indochina.

Led by able rulers, there followed more than a century of internal peace and prosperity, as the Chinese people were able to live in security throughout the land, now that the fierce nomadic tribes of Asia had finally been conquered. However, by the end of the eighteenth century, against a background of tribal rebellions and risings carried out by minority subject peoples, Manchu China fell into a state of gradual decline, exacerbated by corruption throughout the public services.

In the meantime, extensive trade with the European powers had been

"The highest good is the ultimate principle of manifesting character and loving people. The nature endowed in us by Heaven is pure and perfect. The fact that it is intelligent, clear, and not obscured is evidence of the emanation and revelation of the highest good." *Wang Yang-ming (1472–1529), philosopher of the Ming dynasty*

developing since the seventeenth century. Gradually the caravan routes of central Asia began to decline in importance, with the breakup of trading links between Persia, India, and the Far East. Toward the end of the eighteenth century, the foreign powers began to import opium into China from India and the Middle East as a means of paying for their exports, which had previously been paid in silver. By the 1830s, opium imports had overtaken Chinese exports in tea and silk; the subsequent drain on the Chinese economy weakened the Manchu state even further.

At the beginning of the seventeenth century, Asia was the most densely populated and richest continent in the world, yet despite its wealth and territorial size, these vast empires began to decline in terms of progress and technological advancement. They were less well organized than the European states, who saw in them lands open for rich pickings, trade, and eventual colonization.

A British merchant ship engaged in the opium trade, anchored off Lin Tin, southern China, c. 1834.

CHINESE EXPANSION DURING THE MING DYNASTY

Despite the tremendous destruction caused to China by Mongol conquests in the fourteenth century and especially by the Mongol Yüan dynasty between 1280 and 1367, the Mongols were overthrown by a new dynasty, the Ming, led by its founder, Chu Yüan-chang, who took power in Nanking in 1368, aiming to rule like his T'ang and Sung predecessors.

At the end of the fourteenth century, the Ming strove to restore normal life by reviving agriculture, breaking the power of large landowners and encouraging small peasants. They developed improved agricultural techniques, irrigation works, and new canal system that linked the Yangtze with Peking, the new capital, thus stimulating Chinese trade.

In the meantime, the Ming reformed the army, establishing self-sufficient military colonies on the frontiers. The Ming government abandoned the use of paper money, which had been abused previously by the Mongols, causing damage to the Chinese economy. Throughout the sixteenth century, industry, especially in the areas of textiles, tea, and ceramics, flourished in the great cities, thus stimulating the commerce and trade of the Yangtze Delta— Nanking, Suchou, Wu-shi, Sung-chiang, and Hangchou.

The Ming carried out an aggressive foreign policy with campaigns against the Mongols, with General Ch'in-Fu's expedition in 1409 and those of Yung-lo in 1410 and 1424. Throughout the fifteenth century, the Ming gradually consolidated their power, both within China and with their expansion to the southwest. They had already subjugated Korea in 1392 and occupied Vietnam between 1407 and 1427. The Ming then extended Chinese empire into Korea, Mongolia, and Turkestan in the north and deeper into Vietnam and Burma in the south. Arguably, they had a greater influence in East Asia than any other indigenous Chinese dynasty.

This shows the first issue of paper money, a Ming dynasty banknote from 1374.

Attempts were made to invade Mongolia, but these failed with the emperor's capture in 1449, putting the Ming back on the defensive. Mongol pressure continued, especially under Altar Khan (1550–1573), and later, in 1556, the Mongols advanced on Peking, only to be repulsed. Throughout the sixteenth century, the Chinese were also constantly harassed by pirates based in Japan and by the Japanese invasions of Korea by Hideyoshi Toyotomi in the last decade of the sixteenth century. Against this background, Portuguese merchants began to establish themselves in Macao between 1514 and 1552.

Consequently, despite an earlier aggressive foreign policy and the voyages of Cheng Ho-tu in the Indian Ocean, to the East African coast and the East Indies, Arabia, Persia, India, and Java, in the first three decades of the fourteenth century, trade and cultural contacts with the outside world were generally discouraged in favor of developing agricultural wealth and internal trade and communications. The accent was clearly upon Chinese self-sufficiency during the Ming period, in what can be described as a conservative and inward-looking atmosphere.

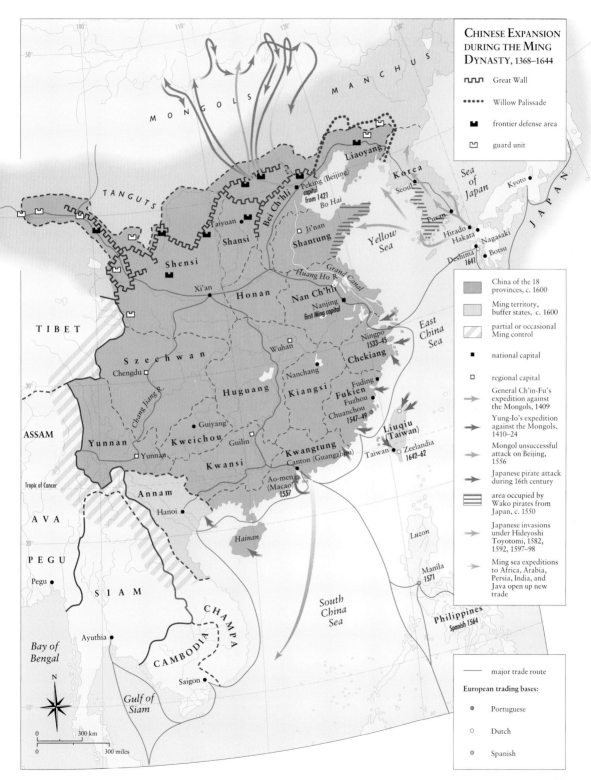

CHINESE EXPANSION DURING THE MING DYNASTY, 1368–1644

ЛЛЛ Great Wall

•••••• Willow Palissade

■ frontier defense area

⊔ guard unit

China of the 18 provinces, c. 1600

Ming territory, buffer states, c. 1600

partial or occasional Ming control

■ national capital

□ regional capital

→ General Ch'in-Fu's expedition against the Mongols, 1409

→ Yung-Io's expedition against the Mongols, 1410–24

→ Mongol unsuccessful attack on Beijing, 1556

→ Japanese pirate attack during 16th century

≡ area occupied by Wako pirates from Japan, c. 1550

→ Japanese invasions under Hideyoshi Toyotomi, 1582, 1592, 1597–98

→ Ming sea expeditions to Africa, Arabia, Persia, India, and Java open up new trade

— major trade route

European trading bases:

● Portuguese

○ Dutch

● Spanish

MONGOLS

MANCHUS

TANGUTS

Liaoyang

Korea

Seoul

Sea of Japan

Kyoto

JAPAN

Peking (Beijing) capital from 1421

Bo Hai

Pusan

Hirado

Hakata

Nagasaki

Deshima 1641

Botsu

Bei Ch'ili

Taiyuan

Shansi

Ji'nan

Shantung

Yellow Sea

Shensi

Xi'an

Honan

Huang Ho R.

Grand Canal

Nan Ch'hli

Nanjing first Ming capital

East China Sea

TIBET

Szechwan

Chengdu

Wuhan

Huguang

Nanchang

Kiangsi

Ningpo 1533–45

Chekiang

Fuding

Fukien

Fuzhou

Chuanchou 1547–49

Liuqiu (Taiwan)

Taiwan

Zeelandia 1642–62

ASSAM

Yunnan

Kweichou

Guiyang

Guilin

Kwangtung

Canton (Guangzhou)

Ao-men (Macao) 1557

Luzon

AVA

Yunnan

Kwansi

PEGU

Pegu

Annam

Hanoi

Hainan

Manila 1571

Tropic of Cancer

SIAM

CHAMPA

South China Sea

Philippines Spanish 1564

Bay of Bengal

Ayuthia

CAMBODIA

Saigon

N

Gulf of Siam

0   300 km

0   300 miles

THE CONQUESTS OF TAMERLANE

The rise to power of Tamerlane (otherwise known as Timur Lenk—Timur "the Lame") marked the end of the Mongol age of conquest. Tamerlane was not, strictly speaking, a nomad but was of Turkish origin from Turkestan rather than of Mongol background. As such, he came from the civilized Islamic society of Transoxania. In 1370, he came to power as King of Transoxania by assassinating his associate, Mir Husein, upon which he declared his inheritance from Ghenghis Khan.

Although the Mongol empire had once been unified, by the time that Tamerlane came to power, toward the end of the fourteenth century, that unity had splintered into the rule of separate khanates in the Chagatai, the Golden Horde, and Persia.

Once he had established his power base in his capital, the wealthy trading city of Samarkand, Tamerlane struck out, fighting a succession of campaigns against his neighbors, establishing local supremacy. He then waged wars against Georgia, Turkestan, and Armenia, conquering a vast Asian empire that stretched from

THE CONQUESTS OF
TAMERLANE (TIMUR)

- maximum extent of Tamerlane's empire, c. 1400
- Tamerlane's campaigns
- city pillaged or destroyed by Tamerlane

Inheriting the Mongol ability to field fast-moving armies, Tamerlane organized lightning campaigns, the backbone of which was provided by his cavalry, similar to that portrayed in this Arabic illustration.

southern Russia to Mongolia and southward to Afghanistan, the Hindu Kush, northern India, Persia, and Mesopotamia.

Tamerlane occupied Azerbajan in 1385 he took Sultaniya in 1390 and Baghdad in 1393. In 1398, he penetrated India through the Punjab, as far as Delhi, where he massacred the population and pillaged the city. This would become his trademark, and he became known to history for his destructiveness. Later, in 1402, his armies swept through Asia Minor, defeating the Ottoman Turks led by Sultan Bayazid, taking Aleppo and sacking Damascus. Although, in capturing Damascus, Tamerlane ensured that all the artists, musicians, and artisans in the city were safely exiled to Samarkand, where they would enrich his capital, he nevertheless ordered the massacre of the rest of the population. He later attacked the Russian principalities and dukedoms, advancing almost as far as Moscow.

Yet Tamerlane's empire was short-lived. He won the battles, but lost the peace, by failing to consolidate his victories, or winning the hearts and minds of the conquered populations and by establishing any form of sound imperial administration. Although he was interested in the arts and reputed to be a cultured individual, he was first and foremost a military commander and an intrepid warrior; he was a conqueror rather than an emperor. Tamerlane was a devout Muslim, who paradoxically ruined all the Muslim empires of his period. His empire had never been a cohesive entity, and after he died in 1405, while leading an expedition against Ming China, his empire soon fell apart. By turning on the khanates, Tamerlane had unwittingly destroyed Mongol power. The Chagatai khanate was destroyed on his death, and the Golden Horde would fall apart by 1502.

EXPANSION OF THE OTTOMAN TURKS

The rise to power of the Ottoman Turks, who had unified the Turks under the Osmanli dynasty, owed much to the weakness of neighboring empires, particularly the damage that had been done to Byzantium during the Fourth Crusade of 1204, which greatly aided Ottoman incursions into southeast Europe throughout the fourteenth century. Likewise the Ottoman bid for power was assisted by the defeat of the Seljuks at the battle of Ksedag in 1243, which subsequent to Mongol withdrawal created a power vacuum throughout Anatolia and Persia. The Ottoman state gradually expanded under Orkhan (c. 1324–1362), Sultan Murad (1360–1389), and Bayezid I (1389–1402). This was the period of continuous Ottoman expansion, achieved through warfare, alliances, and the purchase of territory.

In 1326, the town of Bursa was transformed into the Ottoman capital, and by 1345, with the appropriation of the Karasai emirate, the Ottomans came into contact with the Dardanelles. Led by Osman's son Orkhan, they crossed to Gallipoli in 1355 and gained a foothold in Europe.

The growth of Ottoman power attracted the attention of the Mongol leader Tamerlane, who momentarily turned his attention from conquering India to protecting his western frontier. Subsequently he defeated the Ottoman army at Ankara in 1402. But this was only a minor setback to Ottoman ambitions, since Tamerlane, in true nomad fashion, soon returned to other campaigns without consolidating his victory.

Meanwhile, in Europe Thrace was soon overrun, and in the 1370s, Adrianople, the northern part of Greece, and Macedonia were duly occupied. Later the Serbian nobility, led by Prince Lazar, was heavily defeated at the battle of Kosovo Polje (The Field of Blackbirds) on June 28, 1389, and by the end of May 1453, Constantinople, the capital of the "rump" empire of Byzantium, fell to Sultan Mehmet II, to be followed by Morea, Trebizond, Bosnia, Albania, and the Crimea. Under Mehmet II Crusader armies had also been defeated at Varna in 1444.

Ottoman expansion continued under Selim I (1512–1520), who defeated the

Mamelukes in 1517, effectively doubling the size of his empire by adding Syria, Palestine, Egypt, and Algeria.

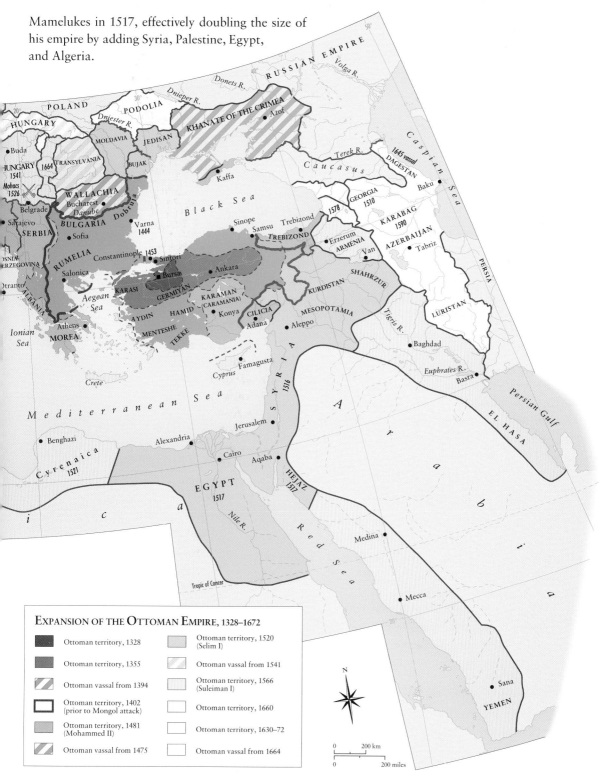

EXPANSION OF THE OTTOMAN EMPIRE, 1328–1672

Ottoman territory, 1328	Ottoman territory, 1520 (Selim I)
Ottoman territory, 1355	Ottoman vassal from 1541
Ottoman vassal from 1394	Ottoman territory, 1566 (Suleiman I)
Ottoman territory, 1402 (prior to Mongol attack)	Ottoman territory, 1660
Ottoman territory, 1481 (Mohammed II)	Ottoman territory, 1630–72
Ottoman vassal from 1475	Ottoman vassal from 1664

0   200 km

0   200 miles

N

DECLINE OF THE OTTOMAN EMPIRE

The "Golden Age" of Ottoman power was realized during the reign of Suleiman I, "The Magnificent" (1520–1566). He defeated the Hungarians at the battle of Mohacs in 1526 and then marched upon Vienna, putting the Habsburg capital to siege with an army of 250,000 men. Despite their strength in numbers, Ottoman forces were obliged to abandon the siege after three days of bitter fighting, and they subsequently withdrew into the interiors of Hungary and Romania.

This adventure into central Europe proved to be only a minor setback to Turkish ambitions. Suleiman next annexed Tripoli, thus dominating the whole north African littoral, and extended Ottoman imperial control southeastward throughout Mesopotamia to the Persian Gulf. The Ottoman navy began to dominate the Mediterranean Sea, which for much of the sixteenth century would be transmogrified, effectively, into a "Turkish lake."

By the seventeenth century, the whole of the Balkan Peninsula had fallen under Ottoman control. Croats and Serbs, exiled to the north of the Sava and Danube rivers, served as frontier troops, protecting both the Holy Roman Empire and Christendom from further Ottoman incursions. In turn, during the next hundred years Austrian forces, made up of a variety of peoples, gradually drove the Ottomans back into the Balkans. Nevertheless, Ottoman counterattacks throughout the 1670s once again threatened Austrian possessions and Vienna.

Ottoman success was not predicated upon military prowess and organization alone, but also upon diplomacy and a policy of toleration toward non-Muslim subject peoples. Christian princes and nobles were often employed in the service of the sultan out of their own concerns and fears of the spread of Habsburg power. Meanwhile the Sublime Porte developed trade with the peoples around the Mediterranean littoral, seizing power and influence from the merchants of Marseille, Venice, and Ragusa (Dubrovnik).

Weaknesses within the Ottoman power structure and society slowly became apparent, eventually leading to the nineteenth century epithet that Turkey had become the "sickman of Europe." Contributing to the Ottoman decay were widespread administrative weakness, corruption, a lack of centralization, and the poor quality of Suleiman's successors. If the sultan's power was enfeebled by growing anarchy and the ambitions of the *devsirme* and the Janissaries, it was further debilitated by the gradual acquisition of Mediterranean trade by Greek, Slav, and Italian merchants. The growing power and influence of Muslim religious institutions from the sixteenth century conflicted with the authority of successive sultans. Conservative in character, the *ulema* class of religious leaders and teachers worked against the forces of modernism.

By the nineteenth century, powerful European states had arisen, and they reacted against Ottoman imperial hegemony. Forming themselves into an alliance system against the Sublime Porte, the European powers gradually drove the Ottomans out of central Europe. Although the Ottoman empire still sprawled across southeastern Europe, Asia Minor, and the Maghreb throughout the eighteenth century, by the end of the century the Ottoman empire, politically, economically, and socially stagnant, was no longer considered to be a serious threat to its European neighbors.

Ottoman Empire, 1683–1914

- territory lost by 1718
- territory lost by 1812
- territory lost by 1881
- territory lost by 1914
- Ottoman empire, 1914
- 1811 — date granted autonomy
- 1830 — date of territory lost

PART V: COLONIALISM

When the Chinese Ming (1368–1644) overthrew the Mongols, rival Asian empires strove for power, throwing Anatolia and overland trade routes into disarray. The Ottoman Turks cut the sea routes between Asia and Europe and conquered Syria, Mecca, and Medina, as well as moving into the Balkans. Persia enjoyed a brief period as a great power under Safavid Shah Abbas. The conversion of Persia to Shi'ite Islam initiated more virulent wars with the Sunni Ottomans; Persia also engaged in trade with the British East India Company. After 1736, Persia weakened and became an arena for European, Russian, and Turkish rivalry and was eventually divided into spheres of influence. India succumbed to the Mughals, who allowed religious toleration and achieved a large degree of unity under Akbar, but later rulers allowed India to fall into warring Sikh, Muslim, and Hindu states. The subsequent chaos permitted Britain and France to commence trade and build empires. All Atlantic European states were reaching Asia by sailing around Africa into the Indian Ocean, outflanking the Ottoman empire to reach the spice islands. After throwing the French out of India, Britain expanded, defeating and annexing states and creating protectorates. By the mid-nineteenth century, they controlled all India. The French, seeking recompense in empire after the loss of Alsace-Lorraine at the end of the Franco-Prussian War, moved into Indochina. Russia expanded into central Asia, bringing her territories close to India, causing the British severe alarm. Elsewhere, Russia reached the Pacific and seized the Amur province from China, this movement being started by merchants, settlers, and ambitious local administrators. As with so many imperial powers, it was often the agent on the spot who made policy decisions. China, too, suffered encroachment, being attacked by Britain and France in a series of Opium Wars and forced to cede Hong Kong to Britain and to grant trade, diplomatic, and political concessions. Likewise, Japan was unlocked when a powerful American fleet led by Matthew Perry secured a consular treaty and opened the ports of Hakodate and Shimoda to U.S. commerce. The lesson being learned was Asia's weakness in the face of superior western military technology. The desire for trade was soon turned into economic and political control; the final important imperialist state acting in Asia was the United States. Although the China and Japan trades were significant to American textile exporters, foreign markets were not essential for U.S. economic survival. The acquisition of the Philippines in the 1898 Spanish-American War can be explained in strategic terms, with the United States protecting her future in the Far East and acting just as Britain had in protecting her Indian interests. Nevertheless, the annexation was legitimized by President McKinley in "humanitarian" terms. There was no alternative "but to take them all, and to educate the Philippinos, and uplift and Christianise them, and by God's grace do the very best we could by them, as our fellow men, for whom Christ also died."

In the last half of the nineteenth century, both mercantilism and free trade became ingredients in a more aggressive scramble for colonies. The pace of imperialism increased, the main beneficiary of its formal and informal modes

being Britain. Expansion into Asia was mirrored by European expansion into Africa and the Pacific. To explain the colonial and imperial experience is difficult; motivations are rich and varied, but theories of imperialism include economic, political, ideological, and psychological forms; these will be examined in turn, although they sometimes overlap. For example, Britain assumed control of foreign countries for commercial and economic reasons, or because they guarded a trade route, or to gain a new market for manufactured goods or to acquire raw materials. First, commercial and economic explanations are highly significant in viewing imperialism. In the early to mid-nineteenth century, Britain preferred not to have authority over territories in order to win trade routes and markets, but was prepared to use military and naval forces to preserve its commercial interests and, when these were threatened, to annex the area concerned (as in North Borneo). In fact, much British imperialism was occasioned by the need to protect Indian trade. The British empire was based on free trade and a preference for informal economic domination. Exemplifying this was the British fear of Russian expansion into Turkey; policy was constructed to capture Turkish trade, and, when Turkish industry declined, Turkey was coerced into borrowing heavily from Britain in a form of financial imperialism and domination. French imperial expansion took a dramatic turn under Prime Minister Jules Ferry, who, in a burst of mercantilist fervor, acquired

The British ship H.M.S. Nemesis destroys junks off the Chinese coast during the first Opium War, 1839–1842.

Tonking for France. French and British competition in Asia resulted in the British annexation of Burma and then a Franco-British partition of areas of Siam. Lands grabbed for obvious economic reasons were small coastal territories such as Singapore, Labuan, Aden, Hong Kong, Kowloon, Cochinchina, and Saigon. These gave command over important hinterlands. When France controlled all Indochina, she claimed special interests in the neighboring Chinese provinces of Kwantung, Kwangsi, Yunnan, and Szechuan. Certain economic theories link imperialism with capitalism and hark back to the Englishman Hobson, but also Karl Marx and Lenin. The latter explained the European expansion during the late nineteenth century as the inevitable result of the need for European capitalist economies to export their surplus capital. Criticisms of Lenin are many and destructive of his views, but nevertheless Lenin was an early analyst highlighting economic motives.

A second series of explanations characterizing colonialism concerns political motivations. By the 1870s, the European balance of power changed with the decline of France and the unification of Germany and Italy. All nations looked at British strength, saw her trade and empire, and wanted their own place in the sun, and

A British trading mission had established itself in Hong Kong in the early nineteenth century.

subsequently carved up the world in a spate of aggressive nationalist imperialism. Britain sought to maximize her profits, retain exclusive control over world markets, and informally subject foreign governments to dependence on British trade or financial investment. In both Asia and Africa, France attempted to restore her failing prestige, renew her self-respect, generate fanatical patriotism, and rival British commerce. The threat to British business and hence her world hegemony ensured that British governments would give a high priority to its defense and furtherance. In the United States, Captain A.T. Mahan's book, *The Influence of Sea Power on History* (1890), predicted a great war with the Far Eastern countries and claimed the possession of a strong navy would grant America victory. Linked to populist politics, American jingoism under President McKinley reached its height with overseas expansion. Hawaii was annexed and Puerto Rico, Guam, and the Philippines acquired in 1898, and Cuba was occupied. Some American expansionists envisaged a line of control from the U.S. East Coast to Cuba, through the Panama Canal to Hawaii, Guam, and Manila in the Philippines. They hoped such a line would equal British power in its chain of Gibraltar, Malta, Suez, Aden, India, Singapore, and Hong Kong.

A final set of explanations focus on ideological and moral motives. According to these, political, cultural, or religious beliefs force states into colonialism and imperialism as missionary activity. Britain's colonial empire was therefore motivated in part by the idea that it was the "white man's burden" to civilize "backward peoples." French foreign policy documents constantly mention her "civilizing mission" and America claimed humanitarian motives when she took the Philippines and Cuba. Apparent in the psyches of imperial states was a feeling of racial superiority and a belief in the social Darwinist survival of the fittest where might is right.

Whatever the explanations of colonialism and imperialism, these movements have been creative and destructive. Traditional institutions were pulled down and modes of thought replaced by western ones as colonizers sought to educate subject peoples into occidental ways. The creation of a western-style educated elite gradually introduced tensions into colonial societies, with the poor observing how their own people were aping colonial masters. On the other hand, the introduction of medicine, irrigation, and more efficient administrative systems would have been beneficial.

Despite the success of colonial trade and imperial policy, the Asian subject

Tea picked in China was initially exchanged for opium and later for precious metals.

Drumming up support for Sun Yat-sen's (Sun I-hsien's) Chinese Nationalist Revolution in 1912.

states fought back in a variety of ways. In 1899, a Chinese secret society, known to the West as Boxers, began a terrorist campaign against western missionaries and Chinese Christians in a nationalist uprising. Many foreigners took shelter in their legations in Peking (Beijing), which was placed under siege. A mixed European and American expedition relieved the refugees in August 1900. The next attempt at ousting western influence was attempted by Sun Yat-sen (Sun I-hsien), whose United Revolutionary League overthrew the Manchus in October 1911 and founded the Republic of China in 1912. He turned his revolutionary party into the Kuomintang and competed for power with the warlords who had destroyed Chinese unity. Seeking to unify the country, he restructured his government following Soviet methods and advocated economic development and democratic republican government. He failed to control much of China and died in March 1925, leaving his successor, Chiang Kai-shek (Chiang Chieh-shih), to pursue his ambitions; he too failed, leaving Mao Tse-tung (Mao Zedong), his Communist enemy, to succeed in unifying China.

Siam retained a degree of independence. Two progressive kings, Mongkut (1851–1868) and Chulalongkorn (1868–1910), engaged in internal reform and reorganized the government efficiently. A policy of relinquishing Siamese rights in Cambodia to the French, allowing foreign consulates with extraterritoriality rights, and ceding border areas to French Cambodia and British Malaya, ensured independence for the remainder of Siam. The development of commercial rice farming and improved tax collection methods allowed Siam to grow stronger. A surprising event was Siam's joining the Allies in 1917 in the First World War.

French colonial rule in Indochina was characterized by inconsistency, autocracy, and centralization, and economic exploitation for the benefit of France. Economic progress allowed the French and a small group of rich Vietnamese to reap rewards. The poor and deprived could not buy land in the Mekong Delta, which was opened up by irrigation works, and ended up as landless tenants. Other peasants became forced labor, reflecting the general lack of civil liberties under French rule. The French excluded Vietnamese from modern areas of the economy, and a particular view became prevalent that capitalism was foreign and the French should be thrown out. Troublesome uprisings gathered apace, and clandestine nationalist movements developed. One nationalist leader, Phan Boi Chau, incited anti-French agitation but was forced into exile. In 1930, another revolutionary leader, Nguyen Thai Hoc, was beheaded, and thousands of his supporters were imprisoned in concentration camps. Vietnam had to wait until Ho Chi Minh for a successful revolutionary.

Japan prevented foreign domination by using a dynamic modernization program, initiating aspects of the West and adopting technology and military reforms (copying British and German methods). This policy gained Formosa (Taiwan) in 1895. The strength of Japan grew so that she too became a colonizer, increasing her prestige by defeating the mighty Russian empire in 1905, and then annexing Korea.

The British empire in India was important as a symbol of world power and for trade and military reasons. The 1857 Sepoy Mutiny was the first large-scale rebellion against Britain; later, Indians who had studied abroad developed nationalist propaganda campaigns in the Hindu press and created secret political organizations. The most important group was the Indian National Congress, founded in 1885, which included both Hindus and Muslims in its membership.

Japan's success against Russia demonstrated what Asians could achieve and encouraged radical nationalists to engage in terrorist campaigns. In India, after the First World War, Britain suspended civil rights and used martial law in rioting areas. During this period, Gandhi became an important leader and asked Indians to face British authority with passive resistance. Demonstrations followed, and troops fired into the crowds at Amritsar, causing hundreds of casualties. This massacre developed noncooperation as an art form. Boycotts of British goods and institutions ensued, with some violence despite Gandhi's call for nonviolence. By the 1930s, Indians were protesting at the government salt monopoly, and riots occurred in Calcutta and Delhi. Muslim leaders outside the Congress feared Hindu domination would arise out of any negotiations with the British, and this added another layer of misery, with Hindu-Muslim clashes. Finally, in 1935, a Government of India Act was passed in the British parliament establishing autonomous legislative bodies in the provinces and a two-chamber legislature. Gandhi approved this result of Indian revolt, and the Act became effective in April 1937. However, many members of the Indian National Congress desired full freedom and sovereignty.

THE MUGHAL DYNASTY IN INDIA, 1526–1707

In 1526, Babur invaded India from Afghanistan and defeated Sultan Ibrahim Lodi of Delhi at the battle of Panipat. Babur occupied Agra, the Lodi capital, and proclaimed himself emperor of all Muslim lands in India. After his death, the Mughals were expelled for a brief period by Sher Shah, but Akbar, Babur's grandson, reinvaded India and proved to be the greatest monarch of the Mughal empire. During his reign (1556–1605), he defeated rebellious princes in the Punjab, Rajputana, and Gujerat. In 1576, he acquired Bengal, conquered Kashmir between 1586 and 1592, and annexed Sind in 1592. Between 1598 and 1601, he subdued some of the Muslim kingdoms in the Deccan with Khandesh, and Berar among them. Many Indian states became tributary allies, most noticeably the Rajput princes, and the empire was divided into fifteen provinces (*subah*), each administered by a new class of bureaucrats, a governor, a revenue and tax office, military commander, religious administrator, and agents passing back information to the central government. An equitable taxation system was introduced, with revenue deriving from land tax and from forests, irrigation canals, fisheries, salt, tribute, and customs duties. Akbar's marriage to a Rajput princess of Amber marked a change in religious policy; the tax on non-Muslims (*jizya*) was abolished, introducing a new period of religious impartiality and conciliation. His reign was characterized by the political, economic, and administrative unification of northern India. Culturally, Persian became the official language, and there was a fusion between Hindu and Muslim architecture (as in the sandstone capital at Fatehpur Sikri), painting, and literature. Architectural excellence is best remembered through Akbar's grandson, Shahjahan, who built the Taj Mahal. Painting originally owed much to the Safavid school of Persia but soon developed its own spirit, the earliest example probably being the illustrated folktale *Tutinama* (Tales of a Parrot).

Akbar had inaugurated an expansionist foreign policy, which was continued by his descendants. Shajahan faced some unsuccessful rebellions and then expanded into the Deccan, where Bijapur and Golconda became tributaries. His son, Aurangzeb, usurped the throne in a fratricidal battle and reversed his predecessor's religious policies, taxed non-Muslims and started anti-Hindu practices that culminated in many rebellions, the most serious being the Sikh uprising in the 1670s. Aurangzeb's destructive policies affected diplomacy, attacking outside India, where he failed to take Assam but seized Chittagong from Arakan. During his campaigns in the Deccan, the Marathas, a warlike people, built an independent kingdom on the Konkan coast from the Gulf of Cambray to Goa. By 1700, Maratha depredations ravaged the Deccan, the Rajput allies were at war, and the Sikhs and Jats rebelled. On Aurangzeb's death in 1707, the empire collapsed. New states, such as Hyderabad (1712) and a Maratha Confederacy, emerged, generating such weakness that the Persians invaded in 1739, while earlier in 1717, the British East India Company constructed spheres of influence, leading eventually to their dominance in India.

The Taj Mahal, the finest example of Mughal architecture, was built by Shahjahan to commemorate the death of his beloved wife, Mumtaz.

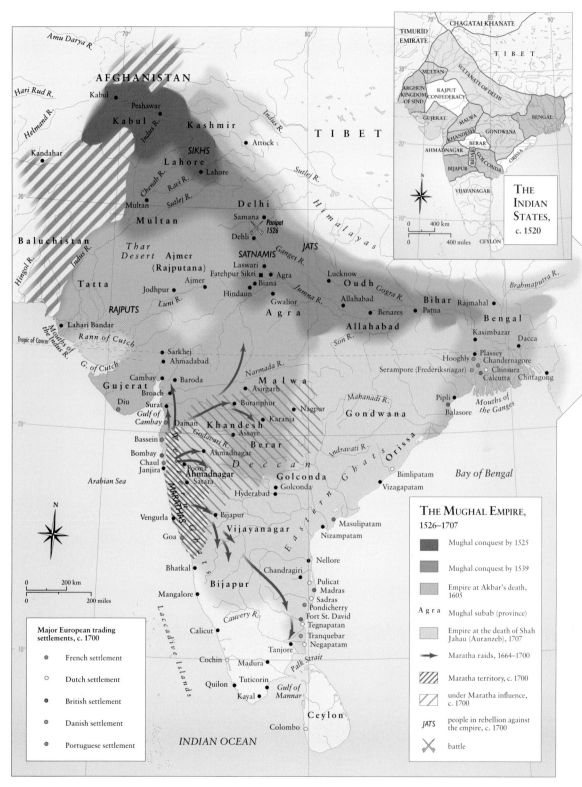

CHAGATAI KHANATE

TIMURID
EMIRATE

TIBET

MULTAN

SULTANATE OF DELHI

ARGHUN
KINGDOM
OF SIND

RAJPUT
CONFEDERACY

BENGAL

GUJERAT

MALWA

KHANDESH

GONDWANA

BERAR

AHMADNAGAR

BIDAR

GOLCONDA

ORISSA

BIJAPUR

VIJAYANAGAR

CEYLON

THE
INDIAN
STATES,
c. 1520

0   400 km
0   400 miles

AFGHANISTAN

Amu Darya R.
Hari Rud R.
Kabul
Peshawar
Kabul
Kashmir
Kandahar
SIKHS
Lahore
Lahore
Attock
TIBET

Indus R.
Chenab R.
Ravi R.
Sutlej R.
Multan
Multan
Sutlej R.
Delhi
Samana Panipat 1526
Dehli
JATS
Himalayas

Baluchistan
Thar Desert
Ajmer (Rajputana)
SATNAMIS
Laswari
Fatehpur Sikri Agra
Jodhpur Ajmer Biana
Hindaun Gwalior
Lucknow
Oudh Gogra R.
Allahabad
Bihar Rajmahal
Patna
Bengal
Kasimbazar
Dacca

Tatta
Luni R.
RAJPUTS
Agra
Jumna R.
Allahabad
Benares
Son R.
Ganges R.
Brahmaputra R.

Lahari Bandar
Rann of Cutch
Tropic of Cancer
G. of Cutch
Sarkhej
Ahmadabad
Cambay Baroda
Gujerat
Broach
Diu
Surat
Gulf of Cambay
Daman
Bassein
Bombay
Chaul
Janjira
Poona
Ahmadnagar
Satara
Vengurla
Goa
Bhatkal
Mangalore
Bijapur

Narmada R.
Malwa
Asirgarh
Buranphur
Karanja
Khandesh
Assaye
Berar
Godavari R.
Ahmadnagar
Hyderabad
Golconda
Golconda
Bijapur
Vijayanagar
Chandragiri

Nagpur
Mahanadi R.
Gondwana
Pipli
Balasore
Mouths of the Ganges
Indravati R.
Orissa
Eastern Ghats
Bimlipatam
Vizagapatam
Bay of Bengal

Hooghly
Plassey
Chandernagore
Serampore (Frederiksnagar)
Chinsura
Calcutta
Chittagong

Arabian Sea
Western Ghats
MARATHAS
Deccan

N
0 200 km
0 200 miles

Masulipatam
Nizampatam
Nellore
Pulicat
Madras
Sadras
Pondicherry
Fort St. David
Tegnapatan
Tranquebar
Negapatam
Tanjore

Calicut
Cochin
Quilon
Tuticorin
Kayal
Madura
Cauvery R.
Palk Strait
Gulf of Mannar
Laccadive Islands

Ceylon
Colombo
INDIAN OCEAN

Major European trading settlements, c. 1700
● French settlement
○ Dutch settlement
● British settlement
● Danish settlement
● Portuguese settlement

THE MUGHAL EMPIRE, 1526–1707
Mughal conquest by 1525
Mughal conquest by 1539
Empire at Akbar's death, 1605
Agra Mughal subab (province)
Empire at the death of Shah Jahau (Auranzeb), 1707
Maratha raids, 1664–1700
Maratha territory, c. 1700
under Maratha influence, c. 1700
JATS people in rebellion against the empire, c. 1700
battle

107

EUROPEAN EXPANSION IN ASIA, 1800–1900

The largest empire in Asia was British India, and Britain always acted to protect its Indian interests. Such acts began in the seventeenth century, when the East India Company started trading during the gradual dissolution of the Mughal empire. Following British-French colonial struggles that began in 1746, Clive's victory at Plassey (1757) helped establish British rule in India. Britain acquired Ceylon during the Napoleonic Wars and strove for hegemony during Wellesley's governor-generalship (1798–1805). The subjugation of the Maratha and Rajput states and the annexation of Burma and the Punjab placed British power across major trade routes. The British acquisition of Singapore (1819), which led to a protectorate over

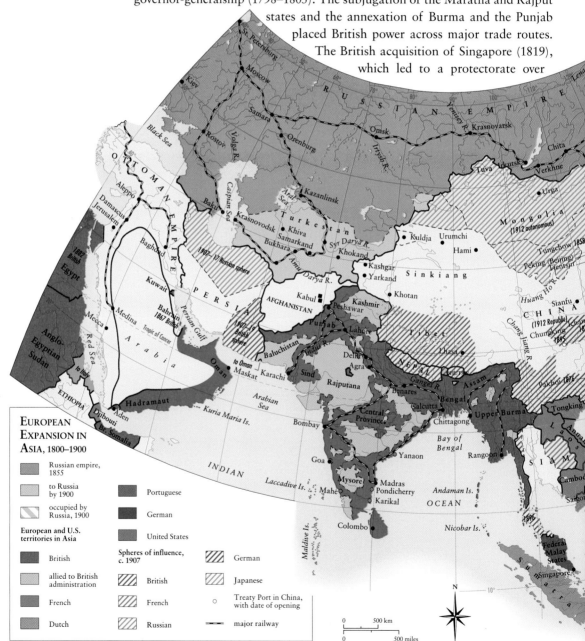

EUROPEAN EXPANSION IN ASIA, 1800–1900

- Russian empire, 1855
- to Russia by 1900
- occupied by Russia, 1900

European and U.S. territories in Asia

- British
- allied to British administration
- French
- Dutch
- Portuguese
- German
- United States

Spheres of influence, c. 1907

- British
- French
- Russian
- German
- Japanese
- ○ Treaty Port in China, with date of opening
- ▪▪▪ major railway

0   500 km
0   500 miles

Malaya (1874) and control over Sarawak, Brunei, and Sabah, ensured control of trade in the South China Sea. The British acquisition of Aden (1839) allowed for the development of a coaling station on the route to India, which became especially important when Britain gained control of the Suez Canal in 1875.

The other two major empires in South Asia were the Dutch and the French. France captured Saigon in 1859 and used it as a springboard to acquire all Indochina by 1893. The colonies were a base facilitating the economic penetration of Chinese Yunnan, a policy aided by the acquisition of a treaty port, Kwangchow. In 1619, the Dutch first established their presence in Batavia through the East India Company. This trading company spread its influence throughout the Indonesian islands, but the Dutch government took over its political rights and benefits in 1799. Under sometimes harsh Dutch rule, peasants were required to devote 20 percent of their land to produce government-designated export crops. Resentment led to the formation of a nationalist movement, Sarekat Islam, in 1912.

In 1899, the U.S. acquired the Philippines, spoils of war from a defeated Spain, and used them to open up Chinese trade. China was subject to incursions by all major imperial powers in the battle for concessions. A series of wars and unequal treaties resulted in many ports, both on the coast and on major inland waterways, falling under European control. China was thus open to the intrusion of western capitalism.

Russia managed to seize Chinese coastal provinces down to Vladivostok and exerted influence in Mongolia and Sinkiang. France and Britain established spheres of influence in Thailand, possibly as outlying bastions to their respective empires. Tensions between European colonial powers took on other forms in the late nineteenth century. Great Britain wished to protect her empire against perceived Russian expansion into Persia and Afghanistan. A 1907 Anglo-Russian agreement allayed fears, and each country took a share of Persia as a sphere of influence. This treaty allowed Britain, France, and Russia to join together in a Triple Entente against Germany and Austria-Hungary.

CHINA UNDER THE MANCHU DYNASTY

In the nineteenth century the Manchu dynasty, weakened by both internal and external influences, reached its nadir. Internally China was shaken by outbreaks of popular unrest, with rebellions taking place in T'ai-p'ing (1850–1864) and Nien (1853–1868). At the same time, China suffered a series of defeats by external powers; in the first Opium War (1839–1842), the Anglo-French War (1856–1858), the Sino-Japanese War (1894–1895), and the Boxer Rebellion of 1900.

The T'aip'ing rebellion took place in south and central China. Its origins lay in agrarian unrest among the discontented peasants, particularly in the Kwangsi province. The rebels established their capital in Nanking and harried government forces for a period of fourteen years, seriously weakening the power and

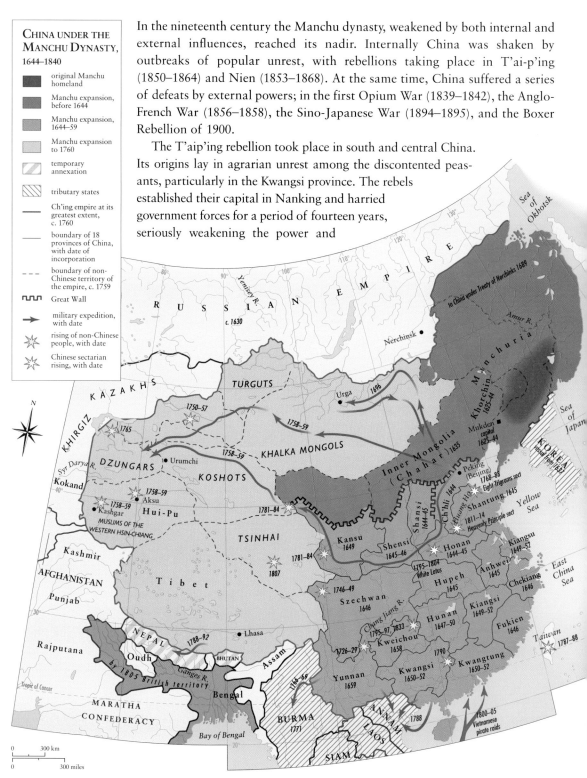

CHINA UNDER THE MANCHU DYNASTY, 1644–1840

- original Manchu homeland
- Manchu expansion, before 1644
- Manchu expansion, 1644–59
- Manchu expansion to 1760
- temporary annexation
- tributary states
- Ch'ing empire at its greatest extent, c. 1760
- boundary of 18 provinces of China, with date of incorporation
- boundary of non-Chinese territory of the empire, c. 1759
- Great Wall
- military expedition, with date
- rising of non-Chinese people, with date
- Chinese sectarian rising, with date

The emperor of China receiving the British ambassador in 1793.

authority of the Manchu dynasty. The T'ai-p'ing rebellion lasted fourteen years, mainly because of the state of anarchy throughout China. Ultimately the rebels were suppressed by government troops, often led by European officers.

In the meantime the Nien rebellion had broken out in northern China in 1852. Like the T'ai-p'ing rebellion, the movement was made up of discontented peasants whose conditions had worsened due to famine and flooding in the early 1850s. The Nien rebellion benefited from Manchu preoccupation with the T'ai-p'ing rebellion farther to the south. Organized into five armies, the movement conducted a series of raids throughout the region. The Nien movement was temporarily strengthened in 1864 by the support of T'ai-p'ing soldiers who had escaped from Nanking when the T'ai-p'ing rebellion was defeated. However, in the wake of the T'ai-p'ing defeat, government forces were ultimately able to suppress the Nien rebels as well.

Earlier fighting had broken out between the British and Chinese over whether or not the Chinese courts had jurisdiction over British citizens who had confiscated opium in Canton in 1839. The war resulted in the British occupation of Hong Kong, which subsequently became a British territory following the Treaty of Nanking. The Chinese were also obliged to pay compensation to the British merchants who had been at the heart of the dispute. At the same time the ports of Canton, Amoy, Foochow, Nangpo, and Shanghai were opened to foreign trade.

Pressure from abroad would affect Manchu China again toward the end of the nineteenth century during the Sino-Japanese wars over the control of Korea, in which the Japanese army, newly modernized along European lines, defeated the Chinese with ease. Similarly, the Russian empire continued its drive to

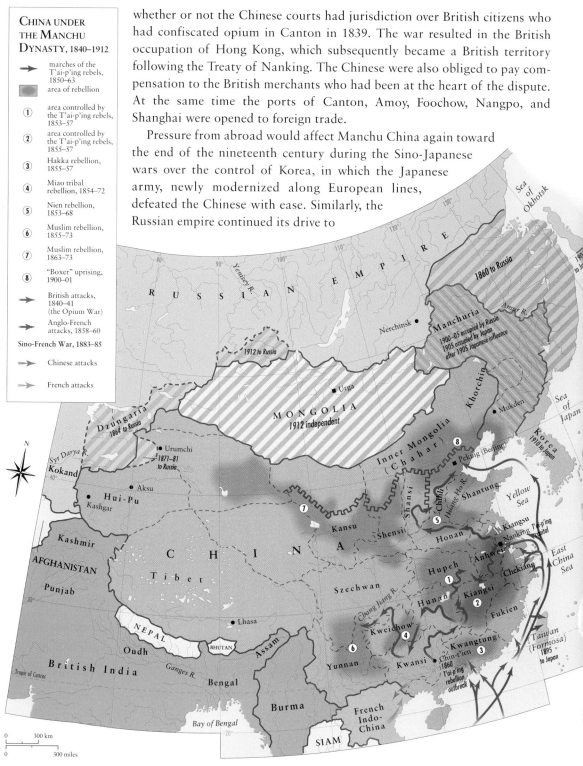

CHINA UNDER THE MANCHU DYNASTY, 1840–1912

→ marches of the T'ai-p'ing rebels, 1850–63

▨ area of rebellion

① area controlled by the T'ai-p'ing rebels, 1853–57

② area controlled by the T'ai-p'ing rebels, 1855–57

③ Hakka rebellion, 1855–57

④ Miao tribal rebellion, 1854–72

⑤ Nien rebellion, 1853–68

⑥ Muslim rebellion, 1855–73

⑦ Muslim rebellion, 1863–73

⑧ "Boxer" uprising, 1900–01

→ British attacks, 1840–41 (the Opium War)

→ Anglo-French attacks, 1858–60

Sino-French War, 1883–85

→ Chinese attacks

→ French attacks

penetrate into Manchuria, sowing the seeds of future conflict with Japan (the Russo-Japanese War of 1904–05).

Resentment against foreign—essentially European—influence came to a head with the Boxer rebellion in 1900. The Chinese were particularly incensed by the German occupation of Kweichow in 1897, the Russian occupation of Port Arthur in 1898, and the British occupation of Wei-hai-wei that same year.

Popularly known as the "Boxers" in European circles, the secret "Society of Righteous and Harmonious Fists" (Yihhe Quai) aimed to expel all foreigners from China by attacking Christian religious establishments and European-controlled railroads in northern China, Shensi, and Manchuria. The Boxers were supported by many in Manchu court circles, including the dowager empress Tzu Hsi (Cixi). The foreign powers responded in force, leading to further anti-alien resentment and fueling Chinese nationalist and republican movements, especially that of Sun Yat-sen (Sun I-hsien).

Ultimately, ruthless economic and political exploitation of China by the foreign powers and the humiliating defeats mentioned above led to further Chinese resentment against foreign influence, at the same time discrediting the Manchu dynasty in the face of competing nationalist and republican forces. Given the background of a general and widespread economic depression, China was on the verge of revolution at the dawn of the twentieth century.

Chinese revolutionary groups began to establish themselves in China, culminating in the Republican Revolution of October 1911, the subsequent abdication of P'u-yi, and the establishment of a provisional government in the hands of Yüan Shih-k'ai.

Revolutionary troops take possession of the Manchu law courts at Chao Tso, January 1912.

RUSSIAN EXPANSION INTO ASIA, 1581–1900

Since the beginning of the sixteenth century, Muscovy had been increasing pressure on the Tatar Kazan khanate and the Astrakhan khanate. By 1556 the entire Volga basin as far as the Caspian Sea was under the control of Ivan IV, "The Terrible"; by 1556, these victories opened the way to Siberia and the East.

Boris Godunov (1584–1605) continued to advance into Siberia, while waging a successful campaign in the northwest and winning back territory on the eastern Baltic coast that had been lost by his predecessor Ivan IV to Sweden during the Livonian war. By 1600, peace had been achieved with the west Siberian khanate of Kuchum, which meant that Russians could expand to the Pacific Ocean. Russian fur traders continued to push the frontier ever eastward, establishing an outpost at Yakutsk in 1632. By 1689, the entire territory to the Pacific, with the exception of Kamchatka, was in Russian hands. Russian aggression in the Amur region soon led to appeals for help at the court of the Chinese Manchu emperor. After a number of bloody clashes, a period of thirty years' peace was eventually agreed between the Russians and the Chinese at Nerchinsk in 1689. The peace treaty lasted for 150 years; a frontier was established along the Stanovoy Mountains that excluded Russia from the Amur River.

Throughout the eighteenth century, Russia continued to add to its possessions in Asia. In 1731, the Kazakhs of the Lesser Horde nominally accepted Russian sovereignty, so that Russian influence spread toward the Aral Sea. Russian sovereignty spread to the Middle

RUSSIAN EXPANSION INTO ASIA, 1581–1900

Russian empire, 1598

acquisitions, 1598–1689

acquisitions, 1689–1725 (Peter "the Great")

acquisitions, 1725–1796

acquisitions, 1796–1855

acquisitions, 1855–1900

Russian sphere of influence in Mongolia and China (1900–14) and in Persia (1907–21)

strategic railways into Asia constructed by 1900

0   400 km

0   400 miles

Horde, although the Russians would not completely control the Khazakhs until the nineteenth century. Meanwhile, to the north of Kazakh territory, settlements were founded at Orsk (c. 1735) on the Ural River, which would serve as bases for further expeditions deep into central Asia.

Between the 1760s and the outbreak of the First World War in 1914, most of central Asia was colonized by the Russians, during a period that witnessed massive territorial acquisition, securing Russia's position as a major colonial power. Moving against the khanates, most Uzbek territory was annexed by the Russians between 1853 and 1855; by 1865 the capital, Tashkent, was in Russian hands. That same year, Bokhara's forces attacked the Russians in Kokand, only to be defeated in 1868, losing their capital, Bokhara. The Russians then annexed Samarkand and the last khanate, Khiva, finally fell to the Russians in 1873.

Anadyr 1762

1800

Nizhni Kolymsk 1644

Nizhni Kamchatsk 1800

Okkhotsk 1648

Sea of Okhotsk

Petropavlovsk

S i b e r i a

Yakutsk 1632
Lene R.

1598

Tobolsk

Tomsk 1604

Omsk

Yenisey R.

Yeniseysk 1619

1689

Irtysh R.

1762

1618

Irkutsk 1652

Chita

1853

1875–1905

Amur Region 1650–1689 To China 1689 Russian from 1858

Khabarovsk 1860

Manchuria

temporary occupation from 1900

U s s u r i

Vladivostok 1860

Sea of Japan

J A P A N

Tokyo

1855

Urga

M o n g o l i a

Peking (Beijing)

Mukden

Port Arthur 1898–1905

Huang Ho

Kaesong

Yellow Sea

1895

C H I N A

BRITISH INDIA

115

BRITISH CONQUEST OF INDIA

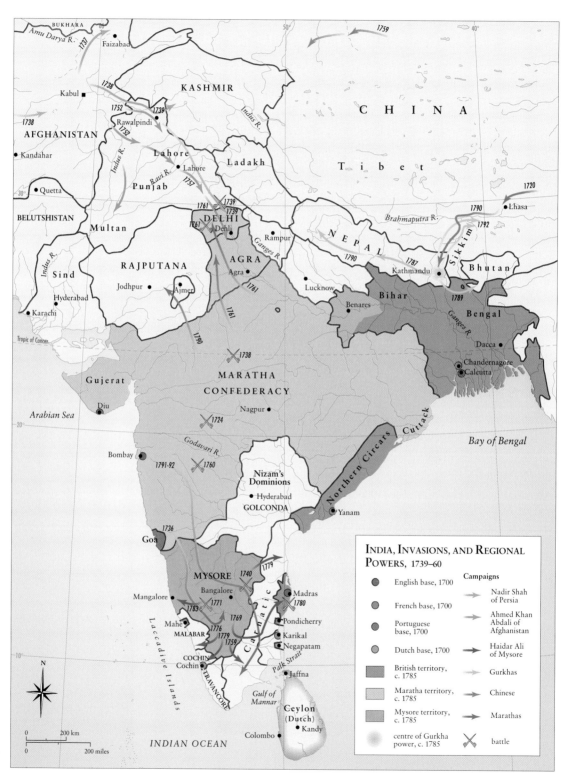

BUKHARA

Amu Darya R. 1737

● Faizabad

1759

KASHMIR

C H I N A

Kabul ■

1738
1752
1739
Rawalpindi
1752

AFGHANISTAN

● Kandahar

Indus R.

● Lahore

Lahore

Ladakh

T i b e t

Indus R.

Ravi R.

● Quetta

Punjab

1757

1720

Brahmaputra R.

1790
Lhasa ●

BELUTSHISTAN

Multan

1761 1739
1739
DELHI
1761
Dehli

1790
1792

Ganges R.

● Rampur

N E P A L

S i k k i m

Bhutan

Sind

RAJPUTANA

AGRA

Agra ●

1761

● Lucknow

Kathmandu ●

1787

1789

Bihar

Bengal

● Karachi

Jodhpur ●

● Ajmer

1761

● Benares

Ganges R.

Indus R.

Hyderabad

Tropic of Cancer

1790

Dacca ●

Gujerat

1738

MARATHA
CONFEDERACY

Chandernagore
● Calcutta

Diu ●

● Nagpur

Arabian Sea

—20°—

1724

Godavari R.

Northern Circars

Cuttack

Bay of Bengal

Bombay ●

1791-92

1760

Nizam's
Dominions

● Hyderabad
GOLCONDA

● Yanam

1736

Goa ●

MYSORE

1740

1779

Mangalore ●

Bangalore ●

1771

● Madras

1780

Carnatic

1783
Mahe ●
MALABAR

1776
1769
1779
1759

● Pondicherry

● Karikal
● Negapatam

Laccadive Islands

COCHIN
Cochin ●

TRAVANCORE

Palk Strait

● Jaffna

N

*Gulf of
Mannar*

—10°—

Ceylon
(Dutch)
● Kandy

0   200 km

Colombo ●

0   200 miles

INDIAN OCEAN

INDIA, INVASIONS, AND REGIONAL POWERS, 1739–60

Campaigns

● English base, 1700

→ Nadir Shah of Persia

● French base, 1700

→ Ahmed Khan Abdali of Afghanistan

● Portuguese base, 1700

→ Haidar Ali of Mysore

● Dutch base, 1700

→ Gurkhas

▦ British territory, c. 1785

→ Chinese

▦ Maratha territory, c. 1785

→ Marathas

▦ Mysore territory, c. 1785

⚔ battle

◉ centre of Gurkha power, c. 1785

The British began to establish themselves in India and imperialistically imported their own architectural style, as illustrated by this painting of Chapra, c. 1796.

By 1696, the British East India Company possessed three fortified trading stations—at Calcutta in Bengal, Madras on the Carnatic coast, and Bombay on the west coast. France also began to trade in India, and the European War of the Austrian Succession (1740–1748) and the Seven Years' War (1756–1763) extended into an imperial contest in India. British successes included Clive's victory at Plassey (1757), and that at Buxar (1764) took Bengal, the most populous area of India. The East India Company wanted no further territory, regarding Bengal as merely a bastion to protect trade. In 1773, the Regulating Act made the Company into a British administrative agency. During the French Revolution and Napoleonic Wars, the imperialist policies of Governor-General Lord Wellesley (1798–1805) were introduced, reducing the Nizam of Hyderabad's domains to the status of a virtual protectorate; Mysore became a vassal, Oudh was cut in half, the Carnatic was annexed, and Ceylon was acquired from the Dutch. British policy was a mixture of force, extortion, bribery, and manipulation, which was targeted at a subcontinent riddled with political and religious disunity. Britain's superior weapons technology, added to a disciplined force of British regulars and company sepoys, placed Indian resistance at a disadvantage. Further wars followed against the Gurkhas in the Himalayas (1814–1816), after which Nepal was reduced in size and became a protectorate, thereafter providing Britain with some of its fiercest soldiers. Central India's state of chaos and lawlessness led to wars subjugating the Maratha and Rajput states. The first Burmese war (1824–1826) gave Assam and Tennasserim in the Arakan to Britain, which conquered Lower Burma in a second war (1852), and a third led to the incorporation (1891) of Burma into British India.

In 1854, Britain met extremely powerful resistance when the Sikhs of the Punjab attacked British positions. This Sikh military theocracy was defeated in 1846 but fought again in 1848, causing extensive British casualties at the battle

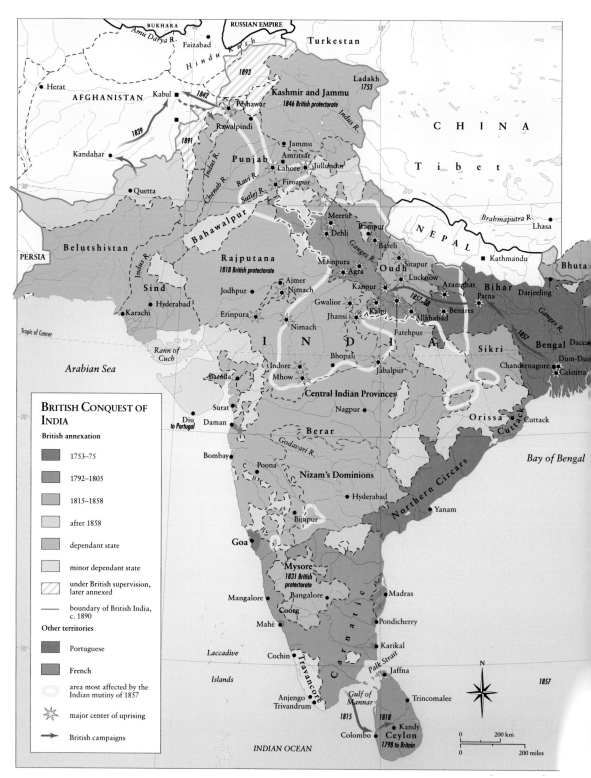

BUKHARA
RUSSIAN EMPIRE
Amu Darya R.
Faizabad
Turkestan

Herat
AFGHANISTAN
Kabul
1842
Peshawar
1893
Ladakh
1753
Kashmir and Jammu
1846 British protectorate
Indus R.
CHINA

1839
1891
Rawalpindi
Jammu
Amritsar
Jullundur
Punjab
Lahore
Tibet

Kandahar
Indus R.
Chenab R.
Ravi R.
Firozpur
Sutlej R.

Quetta
Meerut
Dehli
Rampur
Bareli
NEPAL
Brahmaputra R.
Lhasa

PERSIA
Belutshistan
Bahawalpur
Rajputana
1818 British protectorate
Mainpura
Agra
Oudh
Sitapur
Lucknow
Azamghar
Bihar
Kathmandu
Bhuta

Sind
Ajmer
Nimach
Kanpur
1857–59
Patna
Darjeeling

Hyderabad
Jodhpur
Gwalior
Benares
Ganges R.

Karachi
Erinpura
Jhansi
Kalpi
Allahabad
1857
Bengal
Dacca

Tropic of Cancer
Nimach
I N D I A
Fatehpur
Sikri
Dum-Dum

Rann of
Cuch
Bhopal
Jabalpur
Chandernagore
Calcutta

Arabian Sea
Barcda
Indore
Mhow
Orissa
Cuttack

Diu
to Portugal
Surat
Daman
Central Indian Provinces
Nagpur
Cuttack

BRITISH CONQUEST OF
INDIA
Berar
Godavari R.
Northern Circars
Bay of Bengal

British annexation
Bombay
Poona
C

1753–75
Nizam's Dominions

1792–1805
Hyderabad
Yanam

1815–1858
Bijapur

after 1858

dependant state
Goa

minor dependant state
Mysore
1831 British
protectorate

under British supervision,
later annexed
Mangalore
Bangalore
Madras

boundary of British India,
c. 1890
Coorg
Pondicherry

Other territories
Mahé
Karikal

Portuguese
Laccadive
Cochin
Palk Strait
Jaffna

French
Islands
Trincomalee
1857

area most affected by the
Indian mutiny of 1857
Travancore
Gulf of
Mannar
N

major center of uprising
Anjengo
Trivandrum
1815
1818
Kandy

British campaigns
Colombo
Ceylon
1798 to Britain
0   200 km
0   200 miles

INDIAN OCEAN

British troops recapture a stronghold from Indian "mutineers" in 1858.

North East Frontier Agency
1913–14 to Britain

A s s a m

Brahmaputra R.

Carchar
1882 British protectorate

Manipur
1886 British protectorate

**U p p e r
B u r m a**
*1886 to Britain
formerly Chinese territory*

Chittagong

● Mandalay

1826

**L o w e r
B u r m a**
1857

Rangoon
● Bassein ●
Moulmein
1826

*Andaman Is.
1857*

of Chilianwala. However, defeat in 1849 led to British annexation of the Punjab. Other territories were acquired on the death of native rulers (the doctrine of lapse) such as Muslim Oudh and Hindu Jaipur, Sambalpur, and the Maratha states of Jhansi, Nagpur, and Satara. Under Lord Dalhousie's governor-generalship (1848–1856), India faced an exercise in Westernization, a form of cultural imperialism. Railroads, roads, bridges, and irrigation systems were built; restrictions were placed on slave-trading, suttee (a widow's ritual suicide on her husband's funeral pyre), infanticide, and other traditional practices. He established Western educational procedures that flourished in Indian private colleges, and he planned three universities. Unrest at the acquisition of Oudh, conservative reaction against modernization, the attack on tradition, and the use of English as an official language all contributed to a general uprising known as the Indian Mutiny (1857–1858) whereby Indian troops rallied around the flag of the last Moghul, Bahadur Shah II, as emperor of India. Massacres were carried out on both sides, but the mutiny was eventually ended. In 1858, India became a British viceroyalty, and in 1876 Prime Minister Disraeli made Queen Victoria Empress of India. Hostility to British rule continued, and dedicated nationalists founded the Indian National Congress in 1885.

SINO-JAPANESE WAR, 1894–1895

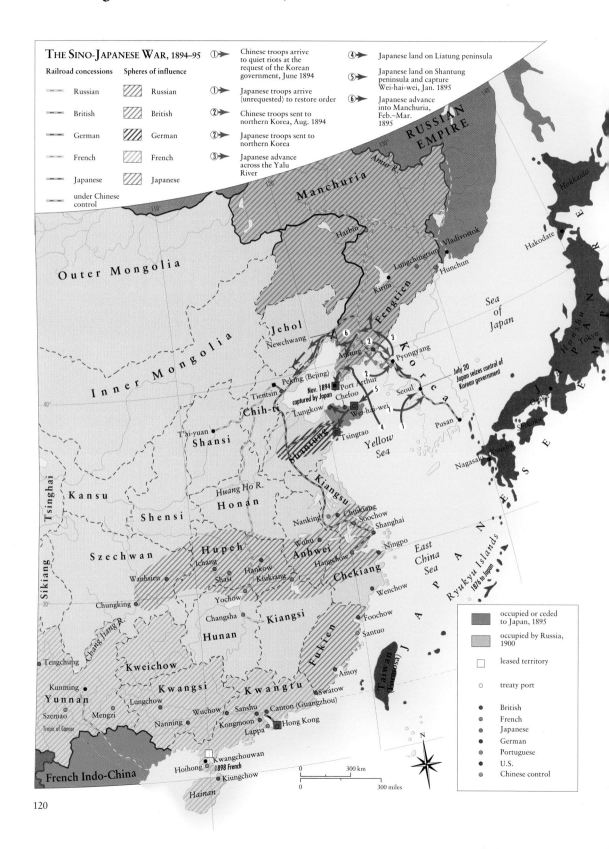

THE SINO-JAPANESE WAR, 1894–95

Railroad concessions

Russian
British
German
French
Japanese
under Chinese control

Spheres of influence

Russian
British
German
French
Japanese

① Chinese troops arrive to quiet riots at the request of the Korean government, June 1894

① Japanese troops arrive (unrequested) to restore order

② Chinese troops sent to northern Korea, Aug. 1894

② Japanese troops sent to northern Korea

③ Japanese advance across the Yalu River

④ Japanese land on Liatung peninsula

⑤ Japanese land on Shantung peninsula and capture Wei-hai-wei, Jan. 1895

⑥ Japanese advance into Manchuria, Feb.–Mar. 1895

occupied or ceded to Japan, 1895
occupied by Russia, 1900
leased territory
treaty port
British
French
Japanese
German
Portuguese
U.S.
Chinese control

The war between China and Japan signified the emergence of Japan as an important world power and displayed Chinese weakness. Conflict between the two states stemmed from the question of which should be paramount in Korea, a Chinese client country. Japanese intervention in Korea can also be categorized as just one more onslaught on Chinese sovereignty and power.

The division of China into spheres of influence with extraterritoriality rights, the rush to extract treaty ports and railroad concessions, all demonstrate the strength of Western and Japanese intervention.

As far as Japan was concerned, Korea was pointed directly at its heart and was potentially dangerous when a client of a latently powerful China or possibly an expansionist Russia. Korea's iron and coal deposits were also attractive to Japan when in the process of adopting Western technology. Japanese industry was being developed by family trusts (*zaibatsu*) such as the Mitsui and Yasuda, and they were pressing their government for access to raw materials. Furthermore, Japan was expanding its territories. In 1875, a treaty gave Russia the island of Sakhalin in return for the Kuriles, while in 1876 Japan occupied the Bonin and Ryukyu islands. In the same year, a Japanese treaty recognized Korean independence, and three ports were opened to Japanese trade. Japan linked itself to modernizing groups in Korea, while China seemed to support conservative interests. In 1894, after completing a successful modernization phase, Japan decided to intervene directly in Korean affairs. A rising of the Tonghak Society in southern Korea elicited a request by the Korean king to the Chinese government for troops to help disperse the rebels. The Japanese regarded this as a violation of the 1885 Li-Ito Convention, whereby both China and Japan agreed to notify the other if intervention in Korea seemed necessary. Japan sent in troops and sank a British steamer carrying Chinese reinforcements to Korea. War was officially declared on August 1, 1894, and Japanese successes were swift. By March 1895, Japan sent troops to Seoul, moved into northern Korea, and then crossed the Yalu River. Shantung and the Liaotung peninsula in Manchuria were seized, and Chinese forces were destroyed. By the 1895 Peace of Shimonoseki, ending the war, China recognized the independence of Korea and ceded to Japan the island of Formosa (Taiwan), the Pescadores Islands, the Liaotung peninsula, and opened four more ports to foreign trade and paid a financial indemnity.

Russia, France, and Germany then intervened and obliged Japan to return the Liaotung for a further financial indemnity.

China's defeat encouraged the Western powers to further incursions, Germany occupied and leased Kiaochow, while Britain acted similarly with Wei-hai-wei. Meanwhile, France grabbed Kwang-chou-wan, and Russia perfidiously seized Port Arthur on the Liaotung peninsula. Concessions were also secured to build railways, and inland waterways were opened to steamers. Other results were: Japan built a large fleet and in response to Russian advances in Asia secured a defensive alliance with Britain (1902) before going to war with Russia in 1904–1905.

RUSSO-JAPANESE WAR, 1904–1905

Rapid political and economic modernization, built upon a surge in industrial and technical development toward the end of the nineteenth century, provided Japan with the confidence to expand in the Far East; Japanese imperial ambitions were stimulated by Japan's victory over China in 1894–1895, which ceded Formosa (Taiwan) to Japanese control. In the meantime it became clear that Russia could not extend its influence any further in the European sphere. Consequently, Russian expansionist policies were also directed to the Far East, where it was believed that a "peaceful penetration" of China would enable Russia to become the dominant naval power in the Pacific. Japan and Russia thus became rivals over Korea and Manchuria.

Following the defeat of China in its war with Japan in 1894–1895, Russia increased its influence in the region with the concession to build the Chinese Eastern Railway across Manchuria, with a second concession in 1898 to build a railway from Harbin to Port Arthur. Russia then turned its attention toward Korea, an area of great interest and concern for the Japanese since it afforded the most direct access to the Chinese mainland. Although the Japanese were willing to negotiate a division of spheres of influence, the Russian government was unwisely contemptuous toward its Japanese rivals.

Japan responded in February 1904 by launching a surprise torpedo attack on the Russian Far Eastern fleet in Port Arthur, causing immense damage. The Russian government was taken by surprise and was left militarily unprepared; the Trans-Siberian railway was still incomplete, and supplies to the Far East had to be transported by boat across Lake Baikal. In the Far East, Japanese troops outnumbered Russian forces and benefited from easy reinforcements by sea. The Japanese held naval superiority and benefit from a number of home ports, in comparison with Russia's two widely distant naval bases of Port Arthur and Vladivostok.

A succession of Japanese victories along the Yalu River and in Manchuria, which included the seizure of the port of Dairen, enabled the Japanese to besiege Port Arthur, which finally surrendered in December 1904 after a siege of 148 days. Russia was left with only one serviceable naval base, Vladivostok, in the Far East. The land war ended with the battle of Mukden, the largest land battle to date, in which the tsar's forces were resoundingly, though not conclusively, defeated.

Meanwhile, Japan continued to benefit from the fighting at sea. Having made an epic global voyage from Reval, in the Baltic, to the South China Sea, the Russian Baltic fleet ran directly into the powerful fleet of Admiral Togo in the Straits of Tsushima on May 27, 1905. Within hours, the entire Russian squadron had been destroyed.

In August 1905, a peace treaty between the two powers was ratified in Portsmouth, New Hampshire. A humiliated Russia now recognized Japan's interest in Korea, which was annexed by Japan in 1910, and ceded to Japan the southern half of Sakhalin Island, control of the Liaotung peninsula, together with Port Arthur and Dairen and extensive rights in south Manchuria.

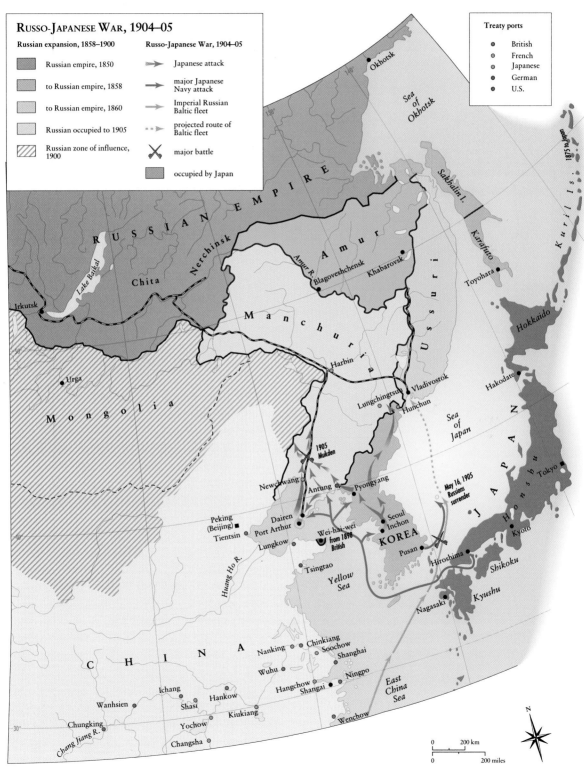

RUSSO-JAPANESE WAR, 1904–05

Russian expansion, 1858–1900

- Russian empire, 1850
- to Russian empire, 1858
- to Russian empire, 1860
- Russian occupied to 1905
- Russian zone of influence, 1900

Russo-Japanese War, 1904–05

- Japanese attack
- major Japanese Navy attack
- Imperial Russian Baltic fleet
- projected route of Baltic fleet
- major battle
- occupied by Japan

Treaty ports

- British
- French
- Japanese
- German
- U.S.

MUSTAFA KEMAL AND TURKISH NATIONALISM

Mustafa Kemal Atatürk 1818-1938, founder of the Turkish secular state.

"Science is the most reliable guide in life."
Atatürk

When the Ottoman armies collapsed in 1918 at the end of the First World War, Constantinople became the center of an Allied military administration. Italian soldiers landed at Antalya, Greeks moved into Smyrna, and the French occupied Cilicia. To Mustafa Kemal, victor at Gallipoli (1915), a former Young Turk and a fierce nationalist, the partition of Anatolia seemed imminent. The emergence of a newly independent Armenia, and Kurdish separatism, confirmed his fears. He organized nationalist congresses at Urzurum and Sivas (1919) that affirmed the unity of Turkish territory, opposed Allied occupation, and condemned the foundation of Armenia. The Nationalists established a provisional government at Ankara, with Mustafa Kemal as president. An agreement with Soviet Russia won military supplies, necessary for defense against occupation forces. The Greek response was to wage war and defeat the Nationalists at Alasehir, Bursa, and Adrianople. The Nationalists were also opposing Sultan Mohammed VI, who adopted a supine and feeble policy by signing the Treaty of Sèvres. The Sultan renounced all claims to non-Turkish territory. The Kingdom of the Hejaz was recognized; it merged with Nejd in 1926. Syria became a French League of Nations mandate while Mosul, Mesopotamia, and Palestine were mandated to Britain. Smyrna, an area of Greek settlement, and its hinterland were assigned to Greece for five years, after which a plebiscite was to be held to decide its future. The Dodecanese Islands and Rhodes were given to Italy, while Turkish Thrace, except for the Chatalya strip, and the remaining Turkish Aegean islands went to Greece.

The Nationalist campaigns to liberate Turkey and revise Sèvres took two forms: negotiation and war. A bloody campaign against Armenia coincided with a Soviet pacification of Soviet Armenia. The Turks took Kars, and the Red Army seized the rest. A peace treaty with Soviet Armenia (1920) ended Armenian independence and consolidated Turkey's easternmost frontier. In 1921, an agreement with France provided for French evacuation of Cilicia in return for economic concessions. A similar compact was made with the Italians. During the summer of 1921, confused fighting between Greeks and Turks continued, the Greek advance on Ankara being contained at the battle of Sakarya. A Nationalist counterattack broke the Greeks; Smyrna was taken in the autumn. An armistice at Mudania (October 1922) allowed for the restoration of eastern Thrace and Adrianople to Turkey, in return for Turkish neutralization of the Straits under international control. The Treaty of Lausanne (1923) confirmed the situation, returned the islands of Imbros and Tenedos to Turkey, and ended reparations. October 1923 saw the proclamation of the Turkish Republic, with Mustafa Kemal elected president continuously until his death in 1938. The president sought to westernize and secularize Turkey by dissolving dervish orders, banning the fez, abolishing the caliphate, making civil marriage compulsory, introducing the Latin alphabet, reforming education, and bringing in Swiss civil and fiscal law and Italian criminal law. State intervention built up trade and industry. In 1935, Mustafa Kemal was awarded the title Atatürk (Father of the Turks), for his saving and modernizing of the state.

British imperial forces advanced together with their Arab allies through Palestine, depriving the Ottoman empire of large stretches of its Arab possessions.

THE NEW TURKEY, 1926

	British possession, 1914
	British mandate, 1920
	under British protection, 1914
	French mandate, 1920
	Italian possession
	Ottoman empire, 1914
	Turkey after the Treaty of Sèvres, 1920
	temporary Italian occupation (to 1921)
	area ceded by U.S.S.R., 1921
→	Turkish campaign, 1920–23
✕	major battle
	Turkey after the Treaty of Lausanne, 1923

Adrianople
Istanbul • Uskudar
Gallipoli • Skelessi   Zongdulak
Mudania • Nicoea
Bursa
Sakarya
Smyrna • Eskischir ■ Ankara
Alasehir   Usak
TURKEY   Sivas
Konya
1920–22
to France
Antalya
Gaziantep
1920–22
to Greece   Urfa
Hatay • Aleppo   Mosul
from 1912
to Italy   Latakia
Terr. of
Alawites   Syria   Kirkuk
to Britain
1878 leased   Tripoli • Homs
1914 annexed   Beirut
1923 ceded by Turkey   Lebanon   Iraq
Mediterranean Sea   Damascus
Habbaniyah • Baghdad
Palestine   Karbala   Kut-el-
Amara
Alexandria   Tel Aviv
Gaza • Amman
Jerusalem
Transjordan   Basra
Al Jawf   KUWAIT
Kuwait
EGYPT   Tabuk
neutral zones
Hejaz
1916 independent
1925–26 to Nedj   N   e   d   j   Dhahran
QATAR
Tropic of Cancer   Medina   Riyadh
Aswan
Wadi Halfa   HEJAZ AND NEJD
kingdom from 1926   OMAN
Anglo-
Egyptian
Sudan   Jiddah • Mecca
Asir
Abha
1889 to Italy • Massawa   YEMEN
Asmara   Sana
Aduwa   Mukalla
ABYSSINIA   Aden Protectorate
Aden

Sinope   Black Sea
Trebizond   Caspian
Kars   USSR   Baku
Urzurum   Sea
Armenia
Tabriz
Rasht
Kermanshah
Cyprus
Jask
Persian Gulf
PIRATE COAST   Muscat
Gulf of Oman
Hadhramaut   Arabian Sea

0   200 km
0   200 miles

REVOLUTION AND INVASION IN CHINA, 1912–1939

"The revolution has established in China Liberty and Equality. . . . Fraternity is the as yet unrealized ideal of humanity. . . . It may be for China, the oldest of nations, to point the way to this fraternity."
Song Ching-ling,
Sun Yat-sen's wife

Japanese troops march along a village street in Manchuria (Manzhouguo) in 1931.

In the aftermath of the Sino-Japanese War, foreign imperialism, matched by dynastic decline, led to the development of two significant political movements in China. One was the constitutional reform movement of K'ang Yu-Wei (1858–1927), who advocated the reorganization of Chinese administrative institutions; the other was the revolutionary movement, led by the founder of the Kuomintang (Guomindang), Dr. Sun Yat-sen (1866–1925), who demanded the abolition of the Manchu dynasty and an end to foreign rule, influence, and intervention in China. It was Sun Yat-sen who eventually came to power by completely overthrowing the imperial house and replacing it with a republic in 1912, thus bringing to an end more than two thousand years of rule by imperial dynasties.

Bitter political struggles followed on the heels of the foundation of the republic, which failed to introduce unity, stability, peace, and democratic change. Internal unrest was demonstrated by the so-called "Second Revolution" of 1913, during which seven provinces declared their independence. These were quickly put down by the military leader Yüan Shih-k'ai (1859–1925), who eventually replaced Sun Yat-sen and ruled China as a virtual dictator.

China was in a very weak position, exacerbated by internal factional dispute, an unstable government, and huge foreign debts. More threatening to Chinese security were Japanese expansionist plans, and in 1915 Yüan was obliged to concede to a Japanese ultimatum, the Twenty-One Demands, which extended Japanese hegemony over China and established the Japanese control of Shantung, Manchuria, and Inner Mongolia.

In 1916 Yüan had himself proclaimed emperor against a background of severe opposition; however, he died shortly afterward, and it became obvious that real authority rested with the warlords and their armies in the provinces, with only nominal rule from Peking (Beijing).

Throughout the 1920s a series of destructive wars between the different warlord coalitions and concomitant revolutionary activities resulted not only in millions of casualties but also in the destruction of civil government. Although Chiang Kai-shek (Chiang Chien-shih) would eventually establish his authority over many of these warlords between 1928 and 1937, some would remain in power in the far west of China until the late 1940s.

In the meantime Sun Yat-sen's (Sun I-hsien's) revolutionary party established itself in Canton. From 1923 Sun reorganized the Nationalist Party, the Kuomintang, by accommodating the Communist Party and seeking Soviet aid for the National Revolutionary Army; he became leader of the Kuomintang the following year. In 1927 Sun led the so-called "Northern Expedition," advancing northward from Canton in a bid to wipe out the warlords and their imperial supporters and to unite the Chinese people. Nanking and Shanghai fell to government forces in April that year.

Chiang then turned on his Communist allies in a bloody purge that resulted in thousands of deaths, thus ending the uneasy alliance between the Communist Party and the Kuomintang. In 1928 the Kuomintang took Peking (Beijing). Most of China was by now controlled by

THE 1911 REVOLT

under Japanese influence from 1905

province in revolt

November 4, 1911   date of province's independence

Manchuria (Manzhouguo)

Sea of Japan

MONGOLIA

1912 independent

Fengtien

Chahar

Jehol

November 13, 1911

November 10, 1911

Korea

1905 to Japan

Peking (Beijing)
February 12, 1912
emperor abdicates

Lushun
to Japan

Ningsia

Suiyan

Hopeh

November 7, 1911

Shantung

November 3, 1911

Kansu

Shansi

October 29, 1911

Yellow Sea

Nagasaki

Tsinghai

Shensi

October 22, 1911

Honan

December 22, 1911

Kiangsu

November 5, 1911

Anhwei

November 8, 1911

Nanking
from January 1, 1912
Sun Yat-sen provisional president

J A P A N E S E   E M P I R E

Szechwan

March 11, 1912

Hupeh

October 10, 1911

Wu-chang
October 10, 1911
revolution begins

Chekiang

October 23, 1911

Sikiang

November 22, 1911

Hunan

October 22, 1911

Kiangsi

October 31, 1911

Fukien

November 8, 1911

Formosa
(Taiwan)

Kweichow

Yunnan

October 30, 1911

Kwangsi

November 6, 1911

November 9, 1911

Kwangtung

Hong Kong
1841 to Britain

Macao
to Portugal

Tropic of Cancer

Burma
1886
to Britain

Kwangchowan

South China Sea

0   300 km

0   300 miles

Philippine Is.
from 1898 to U.S.

Indo-China

Hainau

SIAM

1887–98
united by and to France

N

Japan continued its expansion in China. Here, Japanese troops push from Manzhouguo (Manchuria) toward Jeholin, 1932.

the Nationalist government. Despite this, the warlords continued to hold power in their fiefs, so that many provinces remained outside government control.

Chiang also had to contend with the continued threat of Japanese expansionism. In 1931 the Japanese occupied Manzhouguo (Manchuria), a rich province in the northeast of China, which the Japanese had desired since their victory over China in 1895; by 1933 they had established the puppet state of Manchukuo under the last Manchu emperor, P'u Yi (1906–1967).

Meanwhile, as a result of the purges of 1927, the communist leaders retreated into remote mountainous regions, establishing their own local regimes. The most important of these was the Kiangsi Soviet; it was attacked several times by the National Revolutionary Army of the Kuomintang in 1934, who were thwarted in their attempts.

Obliged to leave the area, some 100,000 people evacuated, led by Mao Tse-tung (Mao Zedong) and the communist leadership on the Long March, a journey of 6,000 miles. About 30,000 survived the journey.

Chiang had turned his attentions to the warlords and the Communists rather than the Japanese, but in 1936 he was obliged to form a united front against a common enemy. War between China and Japan broke out in 1937, with the Japanese marching south to Nanking, the Chinese capital. The war lasted for six years, virtually cutting off the Nationalist government from the outside world. The government was forced to move its capital from Nanking to Hankow, and then to Chungking in central China.

Despite these setbacks, the Chinese people, including the warlords, rallied to Chiang Kai-shek (Chiang Chien-shih), who became the symbol of Chinese resistance. In the meantime the Japanese invaded in force, and by the end of 1938 they occupied most of northern and central China, as well as the chief coastal ports and crucial industrial centers. Although the Japanese were militarily superior and enjoyed both complete command of the air and control over key road and rail networks, the war continued; the Japanese were unable to break Chinese resistance, in spite of the brutality, looting, pillage, and rape, of which the Nanking massacre of October 1938, in which Japanese troops killed 200,000 civilians, served as the supreme example. From 1940 the Nationalist troops were supplied by the British and Americans. Following the Japanese attack on Pearl Harbor, the war became another front of the Second World War. With over two million troops tied down in China, the Japanese were unable to overcome the vast distances and guerrilla attacks on their lines of communications.

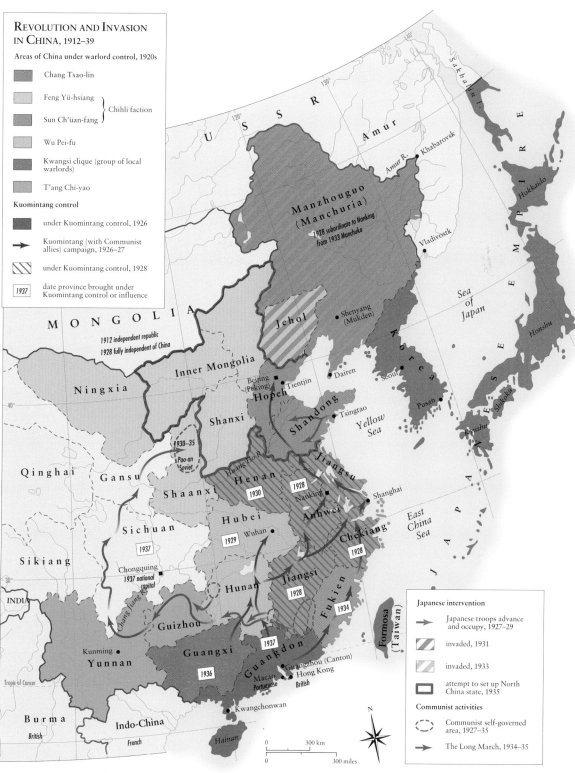

Revolution and Invasion in China, 1912–39

Areas of China under warlord control, 1920s

- Chang Tsao-lin
- Feng Yü-hsiang ⎫
- Sun Ch'üan-fang ⎬ Chihli faction
- Wu Pei-fu
- Kwangsi clique (group of local warlords)
- T'ang Chi-yao

Kuomintang control

- under Kuomintang control, 1926
- → Kuomintang (with Communist allies) campaign, 1926–27
- ▨ under Kuomintang control, 1928
- 1937 date province brought under Kuomintang control or influence

Japanese intervention

- → Japanese troops advance and occupy, 1927–29
- ▨ invaded, 1931
- ▨ invaded, 1933
- ▢ attempt to set up North China state, 1935

Communist activities

- ⬭ Communist self-governed area, 1927–35
- → The Long March, 1934–35

U S S R

MONGOLIA

1912 independent republic
1928 fully independent of China

Manzhouguo
(Manchuria)
1928 subordinate to Nanking
from 1933 Manchuko

Jehol

Amur

Sakhalin I.

Khabarovsk
Amur R.
Vladivostk

Shenyang
(Mukden)

Korea

Sea
of
Japan

Hokkaido

Honshu

Ningxia

Inner Mongolia

Beijing
(Peking)
Tientjin
Dairen
Seoul
Pusan

E M P I R E

Shanxi
Hopeh
Shandong
Tsingtao
Yellow
Sea

Qinghai
Gansu
1930–35
Pao-an
Soviet
Shaanxi
Henan
1930
Huang Ho R.
1928
Jiangsu
Nanking
Shanghai

Shikoku
Kyushu

J A P A N E S E

Sichuan
Hubei
1929 Wuhan
Anhwei
Chekiang
1928
East
China
Sea

1937
Chongqing
1937 national
capital

Sikiang

Chang Jiang R.

Hunan
Jiangsi
1928

Formosa
(Taiwan)

INDIA

Kunming
Yunnan
Guizhou
Guangxi
1936
Guangdon
1937
Macao
Portuguese
Guangzhou (Canton)
Hong Kong
British

Fukien
1934

Burma
British
Indo-China
French
Kwangchowan

Hainan

Tropic of Cancer

N

0   300 km

0   300 miles

JAPAN'S IMPERIAL GRASP

Japan was determined to control an area large enough to provide a defensive perimeter around her sources of supply and her markets, and termed the "co-prosperity sphere." Above, Japanese troops land in New Ireland to secure part of that perimeter.

Japanese nationalism intensified during the Great Depression, fueled by a number of economic pressures. Restrictions on imports and tariffs on Japanese goods were imposed by previous export markets; the silk industry declined; and America closed down the immigration of Japanese nationals, a safety valve for demographic increase. In conjunction with business trusts (*zaibatsu*), the Japanese military devised a plan to establish a sphere of economic domination in Asia to provide raw materials and markets. Accordingly, Japan occupied Manzhouguo (Manchuria) and established the puppet state of Manchukuo in 1932. In 1937, war broke out against China, and Japan achieved several successes, securing territories in northern and central China, although the Chinese never capitulated. In response, the United States cancelled its 1911 trade agreement with Japan, restricting the import of raw materials such as petroleum and scrap metal. Britain and the United States began aid to Chiang Kai-shek (Chiang Chien-shih) and the Chinese Nationalists via the Burma Road, and under the command of Chennault, American aviators, known as the Flying Tigers, fought for the Chinese from 1940. Japanese elites pinned their hopes on the acquisition of petroleum, bauxite, and rubber in the Philippines, Burma, Malaya, and the East Indies. In 1940, Japan forced Vichy France to allow the creation of bases in Indochina.

Japan joined the European Axis in a Tripartite Alliance, and when Nazi Germany invaded the Soviet Union in June 1941, Japan deduced that its Manzhouguan borders were now secure and felt free to act elsewhere. Japanese strategy was based on attacking and weakening the United States, then seizing its economic targets, and finally building a ring of naval and air bases in the Pacific to protect its gains. In December 1941, Japan attacked Pearl Harbor, destroying battleships, but found neither heavy cruisers nor aircraft carriers to bomb. While the Americans were under assault, Japanese armies moved on Hong Kong, Malaya, and the Philippines. Malaya fell within a few weeks, with Britain's remaining troops fleeing to Singapore where they eventually surrendered.

WORLD WAR II IN ASIA, 1941–43

- Japanese, 1933
- Japanese gain, 1937
- Japanese perimeter, July 1942
- major Japanese attacks, 1941–43
- planned Japanese perimeter "co-prosperity sphere"
- British and Commonwealth territory
- USSR and area of influence
- Allied attacks, 1942–43

By May 1942, the Japanese had captured Guam and Wake Island, and American troops were finally defeated in the Philippines when Corregidor fell. In the East Indies, the Dutch capitulated in March 1942. Similarly, British troops were driven out of Burma. The speed of success encouraged the Japanese to extend their defensive island ring by attacking New Guinea and the Solomon Islands to isolate Australia, and also the Aleutians and Midway Island. The Japanese fleet targeting Port Morseby was intercepted by an American fleet in the Coral Sea, and an indecisive encounter blunted the Japanese attack. Midway was protected by U.S. carrier forces, which destroyed four Japanese carriers and many aircraft. This decisive battle was the turning point; thereafter, the Allies seized the initiative and began to drive back the Japanese.

(1) December 7, 1941
Japanese attack Pearl Harbor.

(2) December 8, 1941
Japanese land in the Philippines.

(3) December 8, 1941
Japanese land on Malay coast.

(4) February 27, 1942
Battle of Java Sea; Allied fleet destroyed.

(5) May 5–9, 1942
Battle of Coral Sea; Japanese fleet repulsed.

(6) May 25–June 3, 1942
Battle of Midway; Japanese invasion force defeated.

(7) August 1942–February 1943
Guadalcanal; U.S. forces drive back Japanese invasion forces.

NUCLEAR WAR, 1945

After a fierce struggle to regain lost territory, the Allied powers had driven Japan back almost to its original pre-war borders. Rather than invade the Japanese islands, the fateful decision was made to order an air strike with the newly developed nuclear bomb. The first was dropped on Hiroshima on August 6, 1945, the second on Nagasaki on August 9. Almost at the same moment a huge Soviet army invaded Manzhouguo (Manchuria). In an unprecedented move, Emperor Hirohito announced by radio broadcast Japan's acceptance of the Allies' surrender terms on August 15; the war at last was over.

Although the Japanese were prevented from landing at Port Morseby by the battle of the Coral Sea, they did manage to seize New Britain, Bougainville, Choiseul, New Georgia, and Tulagi in the Solomons. The Allies were faced by a determined and dauntless enemy who had to be pried and burned out of every machine-gun nest and foxhole. The Pacific campaign began in late 1942, when U.S. and Australian forces invaded Tulagi and Guadalcanal. The Allied offensives were hard won; the "Canal" was taken on February 8, 1943, leading to the island-hopping campaign of Admiral Nimitz and General MacArthur in the Southwest Pacific. Landings took place in New Georgia (July 1), Vella-Lavella (August 15), and New Guinea (December 15), and Rabaul was taken in March 1944. This campaign was part of a two-pronged attack. The second part would be a series of landings through the Marshall, Gilbert, and Mariana Islands.

The two advances were eventually to focus on Formosa, cutting Japan off from her southern conquests and resources. Through 1943 and 1944, U.S. forces engaged in horrendous fighting, but by February 1944 they had taken their chosen target islands in the Gilberts and Marshalls. Operations moved to the Mariana and Palau Islands. Saipan, Tinian, and Guam were vitally important targets, being within B-29 bomber range of Japan. American engineers were building airfields on Tinian before the Japanese there surrendered. Now American strategy changed; Formosa was no longer to be attacked; decisions were made to retake the Philippines. Two naval battles sapped Japanese strength, the Battle of the Philippine Sea (June 1944) destroyed several Japanese ships, and the battle of Leyte and Leyte Gulf (October–December 1944) cost the Japanese four carriers, three battleships, and nineteen cruisers and destroyers. Elsewhere, massive Allied air and seapower was then turned on Iwo Jima and Okinawa, which were taken by June 1945 but with considerable U.S. casualties, suggesting that any landing on the Japanese main islands would be extremely costly. Meanwhile, British forces had halted the Japanese advance on India and were moving into Burma, after inflicting heavy losses on the Japanese at Imphal and Kohima. In May 1945, the British Fourteenth Army liberated Rangoon, but remnants of resistance existed until August. British plans to liberate Malaya and Singapore became redundant; an order to surrender was issued to all Imperial forces by the emperor.

Indi

INDIAN

OCEAN

WORLD WAR II IN ASIA, 1943–45

- Japanese perimeter, March 1944
- Japanese perimeter, August 1945
- British and Commonwealth territory
- USSR and area of influence
- major Allied attacks, late 1943–Aug. 1945
- long-range bomber attack on Japan

Japanese defeat was caused by the aggressive capability of the U.S. B-29 superfortress, initially flown from bases in China but later from Iwo Jima and the Marianas. General Curtis LeMay decided on a policy of bombing Japanese cities using incendiaries and napalm. Cities large and small were devastated and coastal waters mined. Debate surrounds the use of the atomic bomb, but one view suggests that losses at Okinawa would have been hugely magnified if Japan proper had been invaded.

On August 6, B-29 *Enola Gay* bombed Hiroshima and on August 9, Nagasaki received the same treatment. The Soviets chose this moment to declare war on Japan and invaded Manzhouguo (Manchuria) and Korea. On September 2, 1945, the Japanese surrendered.

① *June 1942–July 1943*
Operation Cartwheel; Allied forces advance.

② *November 1943–September 1944*
U.S. drive through central Pacific.

③ *February–June 1944*
Unsuccessful Japanese invasion of India.

④ *October 19–21, 1944*
Battle of the Philippine Sea. U.S. Task Force 58 destroys Japanese Mobile Fleet.

⑤ *October 20, 1944*
U.S. forces land in Philippines.

⑥ *November 24, 1944*
20th Airforce begins air attack on Japan from island bases.

⑦ *November 1944*
British offensive into Burma.

⑧ *February 19–March 26, 1945*
U.S. capture Iwo Jima.
April 1–June 1945
U.S. land and capture Okinawa.

⑨ *April–June 1945*
China offensives.

⑩ *August 9, 1945*
Soviet offensive begins.

⑪ *August 6 and 9, 1945*
U.S. nuclear attacks on Japan.

IMPERIAL SUNSET

The Second World War revealed further the frailty of European empires in Asia. Earlier signs of weakness could be seen during Gandhi's civil disobedience campaign, which helped induce the British to pass the 1935 Government of India Act, providing for Indian political participation. Elsewhere, Communist revolts had burst out in the Dutch East Indies (1926), and such militancy exemplified a group of emergent radical, Nationalist leaders such as Ho Chi Minh, Nehru in India, and Sukarno in the Indonesian islands. In the Middle East, a revolt in Iraq stimulated the British to create an autonomous state, and by 1932 Iraq was finally independent and a member of the League of Nations.

The Japanese conquest of Western empires displayed the exhaustion of the imperialists in financial, military, and demographic terms. Furthermore, the Japanese established governments based on local Nationalist movements

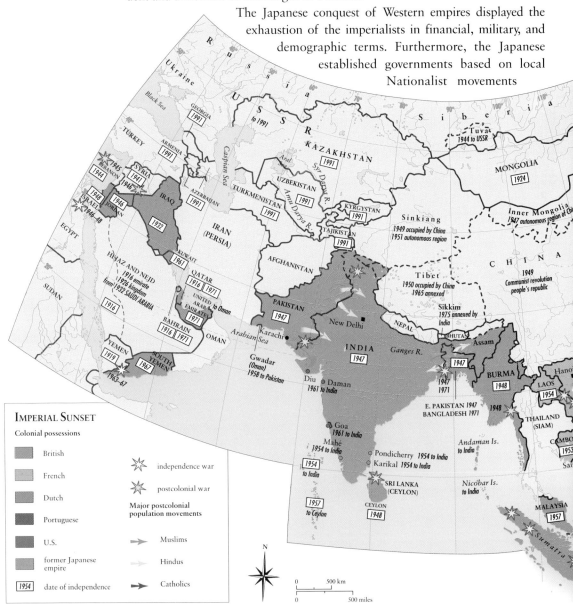

IMPERIAL SUNSET

Colonial possessions

- British
- French
- Dutch
- Portuguese
- U.S.
- former Japanese empire
- 1954 date of independence

independence war

postcolonial war

Major postcolonial population movements

→ Muslims
→ Hindus
→ Catholics

0   500 km
0   500 miles

N

in Burma (1942) and the East Indies and Indochina (1945). Imperial overstretch, accentuated by strong opposition to metropolitan rule within colonies, led to widespread demands for decolonization. Reaction against imperialism articulated itself in a number of ways: indigenous nationalism in southeast Asia and pressure exerted by the United States, who offered a plan giving independence to the Philippines. Additionally, the Soviet Union proffered ideological blueprints based upon class struggle and revolution. Worldwide anticolonialism was also given a forum in the newly formed United Nations, resulting in the uncompromising 1960 Declaration on the Granting of Independence to Colonial Countries and Peoples.

The speed of decolonization was probably occasioned by military weakness and a realization that Europe's shrinking power was now dwarfed by the United States and the USSR. The French and Dutch adopted recalcitrant attitudes toward their colonies and were respectively thrown out of Indochina in 1954 and the East Indies in 1949. Britain was pressured to give independence to India and Pakistan in 1947 and Burma in 1949. Mainland Malaya became an independent federation in 1957, though a Communist Chinese insurgency launched in 1948 was not defeated until 1960. In 1963, Malaya joined with Singapore, Sabah, and Sarawak and named itself Malaysia, but the Malays felt threatened by the large Chinese population in Singapore, and in 1965 Singapore withdrew from Malaysia.

In the Middle East, Britain tried to maintain influence within the Arab world by forming the Arab League and later through the U.S.-backed Baghdad Pact (1955) joined by Britain, Turkey, Iran, and Iraq. However, British credibility had suffered a severe reverse when she left Palestine, whereafter the state of Israel was formed in 1948. Further setbacks occurred after the Suez Crisis, and Britain withdrew from east of Suez. A fierce conflict in Aden led Britain to leave in 1967, and several Gulf sheikhdoms combined to create the United Arab Emirates in 1971. The end of empire in Asia has left independent states to conflict with each other, as with India and Pakistan, or in creating new empires, such as Indonesian claims over North Borneo and Timor.

PART VI: ASIA TODAY

The handover of Hong Kong to China on July 1, 1997, marked the end of empire and the continuing rise of Asia. Hong Kong is one of the first Asian tiger economies, which together with Japan have metamorphosed the image of Asia from one of backwardness, poverty, and failure to that of ever-increasing economic success. The Asian continent symbolizes the future in its dynamic energy and potential marketplaces. In the 1950s, the tigers—Hong Kong, Singapore, Taiwan, and South Korea—were poor, nonindustrial, and economically no different to Pakistan or Latin America. Japan initiated Asian prosperity during this period. Benefiting from U.S. aid and as a base for United Nations–American operations in the Korean War, Japanese politicians and businessmen established the Ministry of International Trade and Industry, focusing resources on heavy industry and technology-intensive products. These were used to increase domestic growth and acquire export markets. New management techniques, a disciplined workforce loyal to the company, and exceptional levels of well-educated students, especially engineers, all combined to secure a modern industrial base. Heavy industry steadily gave way to cars, motorbikes, and electronic equipment. The economic rise of Japan in turn stimulated the tigers to imitate and compete. Certain favorable circumstances have served to facilitate economic success; Japan and the tigers are products of the post–Second World War era and former colonies of Japan or the West. Their political traditions were long since destroyed, and in contrast to the West, especially traditional and established European states, they have had to reinvent themselves while remaining unhampered by past political and ideological baggage. Other factors aiding Asian economies were developing consumer markets in industrialized countries, the ease of technological transfer, and a cheap labor force supplying sophisticated products at a low price. Now Hong Kong and Singapore are two of the most modern and advanced cities in the world; South Korea has a mixed economy exporting textiles, shoes, transportation, electronic equipment, and ships, while Taiwan is well known for its computer industry based on the microchip. Newer tigers have emerged: Malaya, Thailand, Indonesia, and the Philippines; next Vietnam; and now possibly the Chinese supertiger. So successful have the tigers been that Hong Kong and Singapore have higher living standards than many Western countries. However, financial movements during the winter of 1997–1998 show that setbacks can occur, with economic downturns.

The Asian tigers are providing a new model for the developing world, with defining characteristics setting them apart from the old European and American models. The tiger economy is a particular form of state. Very interventionist, the state leaves welfare to the individual and the family. The tiger states are also authoritarian, sometimes even dictatorial, and paternalistic even in democracies such as Japan and Taiwan. These political forms can socialize people into a collectivity, accepting long work hours and low wages for the benefit of all. Hong Kong was no democracy under British rule, with no welfare, limited and expensive housing, and students sometimes attending classes

in shifts due to overcrowding, a legacy being
addressed by the new chief executive, Tung
Chee-hwa. A second feature of tiger societies is
their egalitarian natures, which decry extremes
of wealth despite their existence. Enormous
stress is placed upon education, especially at
the primary level, so all can receive its benefits.
For example, 85 percent of eighteen-year-olds

*The tiny territory of
Hong Kong is now so
successful it represents
the world's thirty-seventh
largest economy.*

are in full-time higher education in South Korea. Their development strategy
and South Korea's economic plans have targeted export-led niche markets and
the development of new technology. A distinctive feature of Taiwan is the
cheap manufacture of the latest invention. This process is helped by political
stability: authoritarianism has been technocratic, efficient, and adaptable. The
tigers are very similar to China, which is not surprising when taking into
account the huge Chinese population living abroad: twenty-nine million
inhabit the four tigers, and the newer tigers domicile another twenty million. In
1978, Deng Xiaoping opened up the Chinese economy with development areas
in the Guangdong province opposite Hong Kong, the Shanghai region, and
Xiamen in Fujian. The Communist Party no longer conforms to ideological dic-
tates and is the guiding and transforming agency for national reform and modernization, reinforced by an interventionist state, an export-focused strategy,
and a commitment to egalitarianism together with political authoritarianism.
Pragmatism marches with the legacy of Tienanmen Square, with economic
growth conferring a degree of legitimacy on the regime. The growth of
Shanghai symbolizes modern China, lying at the mouth of the Yangtze River
with a hinterland marketplace of 160 million people who produce one-third of
China's output. China is the recipient of much foreign investment; in 1997, the
Japanese firm NEC agreed to build a $1 billion microchip plant to open in 1999.
This technology transfer from a multinational company will secure NEC an
extraordinarily large market. Furthermore, in Hong Kong and Shanghai, China
will have access to two leading world stock exchanges. Adding this concentration of power to the heritage of the world's oldest civilization with its ineradi-
cable sense of identity, China's immense size and population mean that the
Asian tigers and Western economies probably will become highly dependent on
it for markets and investment opportunities. The Pacific Rim states will soon
become economically more powerful than the United States; Asia is reassuming
its technical and political dominance, a force to be taken seriously by the rest of
the world.

The year 1997 was the fiftieth anniversary of Indian and Pakistani independence. India was the first great ex-colonial state, with its borders, administration, and politics molded by a British imperial past. Born into a Cold War
world, India placed its future in the hands of a nationalist elite led by Prime
Minister Jawarhalal Nehru. Associated with Nehru are the foreign policy stance
of nonalignment, a model for the decolonizing world, and a multicultural vision

of India. Before independence, Nehru vowed to keep India out of power politics and to link her to the emancipation of colonial and dependent countries. He realized that foreign policy was an outcome of economic policy and that India had to develop to defend herself and work toward keeping peace between the superpowers by mediation and helping the United Nations. So he pioneered nonalignment, which reflected political, military, and psychological judgments about the dangers of the Cold War world. Nehru pursued three styles of nonalignment. Negative nonalignment implied noncommitment to a power bloc, nonidentification with East or West, and nonsatellitism. Positive nonalignment gave India the right to exercise and maintain relations with any foreign country regardless of its Cold War position, provided that this did not entail direct or indirect entanglement in the Cold War. Messianic nonalignment involved contribution to relaxing Cold War tensions and the resolution of Cold War problems in an attempt to create a bloc-free, pluralistic multinational world by helping widen the sea of peace. Here, Nehru was in accord with UN Secretary-General Dag Hammarskjöld's concept of preventive diplomacy. The latter sought to prevent situations developing wherein the superpowers might become involved by keeping them out—the Congo Crisis was a case in point. During the Korean War, India became a mediator and arbitrator in the armistice negotiations and exchange of prisoners of war. India was also a factor in the Indochinese settlement at Geneva in 1954 and was given key positions in International Control Commission teams for Vietnam, Laos, and Cambodia. India has continued to provide troops for UN peacekeeping forces and has led various nonaligned meetings such as the 1955 Bandung Conference, whereby the nonaligned concept has spread to many African and Asian countries seeking decolonization and sovereignty outside Cold War camps. India is now a regional superpower, far superior in population and military force to Pakistan, Sri Lanka, Bangladesh, Nepal, and Burma, but is still presenting an ethos and memory of Gandhi's moral stature. The second main achievement of Nehru was his construction of a new state. India contained many differences and tensions between castes, races, religions, and languages. How then was it possible to build an Indian identity? Religion was kept out of politics, and Hinduism was not to be an element in nationalism. Instead, Nehru pursued an inchoate multicultural identity whereby nationals would assume citizenship along civic and universalist criteria. This phenomenon worked for many years, but now held-back tensions are exploding. In 1956, the Indian states were organized along linguistic lines, a partial response to differences between Hindi and Dravidian speakers. Flare-ups have occurred. On the Burmese border, the tribal hill peoples led by the Nagas and Mizos want a separate state, while the Punjab has seen the birth of Sikh militancy. Nehru's India is now long gone, and probably economic growth is the only policy to alleviate grievances.

Fifty years ago, Great Britain handed the issue of the Palestinian mandate to the United Nations, bestowing a problem to the world that is only now showing some signs of resolution. From the outset, Arabs had fought against the

League of Nations mandate, claiming that the British 1915 MacMahon letter left most of Palestine to Arabs. Jewish settlement and Zionist expansion, together with Jewish migration after the Holocaust, exacerbated hostility. The Arabs rejected the United Nations' 1947 Palestinian partition and invaded the state of Israel when it was proclaimed in 1948. In 1949, UN mediation secured an armistice leaving Israel holding more land than judged correct by the United Nations, with the remainder of Palestine seized by Transjordan and Egypt, the former acquiring the West Bank and the latter the Gaza Strip. A major result of war was a huge refugee problem, with some three-quarters of a million Palestinians fleeing Israel. The Middle East dispute then became a playground for superpower rivalry when Cold War ideological confrontation was inserted into the region, bolstering up each side's client states, although sometimes the tail wagged the dog. A series of wars has followed the 1949 armistice, raising a whole series of issues. In 1956, Egypt seized and nationalized the Suez Canal. British, French, and Israeli collusion secured the military defeat of Egypt, but UN and American pressure prized out the invaders. A UN Emergency Force (UNEF) was placed in Sinai to police the border and at Sharm el Sheikh, allowing Israel to use the sea route to Eilat for the first time. In 1967, Egyptian president Nasser demanded UNEF's withdrawal, reoccupied Sharm el Sheikh, and moved a large army up to the Israeli border. In June 1967, Israel launched a pre-emptive strike against Egypt, Syria, and Jordan to secure more defensible borders and to open up the southern seaway. Victory gave Israel the West Bank, the Golan Heights, Sinai, and the Gaza Strip, and a huge Palestinian population to control. The seventies saw the Palestinian Liberation Organization attack Israeli and international targets; the 1972 killing of Israeli athletes at the Munich Olympics was the PLO's most newsworthy action. October 1973 saw Egypt and Syria start the Yom Kippur War, and an Arab OPEC oil embargo pushed up oil prices. Arab defeat ultimately led to the Camp David Accords and Israeli withdrawal from Sinai. The construction of Israeli settlements on the West Bank generated intense hostility toward Israel; the Palestinians replied with the 1987 intifada. Palestinian problems were worsened in 1990 when Iraq invaded Kuwait to seek financial recompense after being bankrupted by an eight-year war with Iran; Palestinians who had settled in Kuwait were displaced. The Palestinian problem appears intractable, involving land, borders, property, maritime rights, intense rhetoric, and unstable political situations. Nevertheless, the Gulf War prodded the United States to encourage the restoration of Israeli-Palestinian talks at Madrid in 1991. Peace between Jordan and Israel was signed in 1994 after Israel withdrew from Jericho and the Gaza Strip, the administration of these being given to Arafat's PLO. Accords at Oslo eventually led to the January 1997 Hebron Agreement, calling for Israel to withdraw from Hebron and hand over civil powers and responsibilities to Palestinians. The road to peace is thorny, with the Israeli and Palestinian leaders being chained by hard-liners in their electorates, thereby delaying further progress. Nevertheless, the peace process is apparently working. Obstacles emerge, but they are gradually surmounted.

COMMUNISM IN CHINA AND THE KOREAN WAR

The end of the Second World War found China divided between the Nationalist forces of Chiang Kai-shek and the Communist army of Mao Tse-tung, who had overrun most of the northern provinces when Japanese resistance collapsed. By October 1945, Nationalists and Communists were fighting in North China, each side aiming at the control of Manzhouguo (Manchuria). The United States sent General George Marshall to mediate their differences, but to no avail. Truces broke down, and the civil war spread over the country. In the midst of

COMMUNISM IN CHINA

occupied by Communist armies at beginning of Civil War, 1945–47

area of Communist guerilla activity, 1945–49

occupied by June 1947

occupied by 1950

advance by Communist forces

Nationalist attack, 1947

withdrawal of Nationalist government to Taiwan

Nationalist territory, 1950

conflict, Chiang Kai-shek was elected president of China (October 1946) by his party, the Kuomintang. Despite early victories, the Nationalists lost Manzhouguo by the end of 1947. During 1948, Chiang Kai-shek's forces declined rapidly, and the Communists took over most of northern China. The Nationalists were riddled with corruption, resulting in huge quantities of American equipment being sold or surrendered to the Communists. Through 1949, the Nationalist armies collapsed. Communist forces spread throughout the rest of China and drove the Nationalists off the mainland to Taiwan (Formosa).

October 1, 1949, saw the proclamation of the People's Republic of China, with Mao Tse-tung as chairman of the country's administrative council and Chou En-lai as premier and foreign minister. China rounded off its territories by occupying Hainan and invading Tibet in 1950. In 1955, the Soviet Union evacuated the naval base of Port Arthur, which it had seized from Japan during the Second World War. China's first foreign policy activity took place in Korea. The 1945 Japanese surrender in Korea led to Soviet and U.S. occupation. The former established a Communist regime in the north (north of the 38th parallel), suppressing all opposition. After the occupying forces withdrew, North Korea invaded the South in June 1950. Being heavily armed by the Soviet Union, the North's forces rapidly captured Seoul. When American troops were sent in under a UN mandate, they and their South Korean allies were pushed back to the Pusan bridgehead. In September, fresh UN and Commonwealth forces arrived, landing at Pusan and behind North Korean lines at Kunsan and Inchon, cutting Communist communications. Led by General MacArthur, UN (mainly U.S.) troops drove north over the 38th parallel with the express purpose of capturing North Korea and unifying the two halves. The United Nations' subsequent advance to near the Chinese border occasioned a massive Chinese reaction; afraid for Manzhouguo, nearly 200,000 Chinese soldiers crossed the Yalu River and drove MacArthur south of Seoul. The use of massive airpower enabled the United Nations to advance back to the 38th parallel, where the front stabilized in July 1951. An armistice was concluded in 1953 after Stalin's death, the front line becoming the border. The virulence of the war, resulting in the death of some 2.9 million people, can perhaps be explained not just by Chinese suspicion of the United Nations (the West) but also by U.S. and British memories of appeasing Hitler; force just had to meet aggression.

KOREAN WAR

→ North Korean attack, June–Sept. 1950

→ United Nations campaign, Sept.–Oct. 1950

→ Chinese intervention, Nov. 1950

---- armistice of Panmunjan, July 27, 1953, had been effectively front line from July 1951

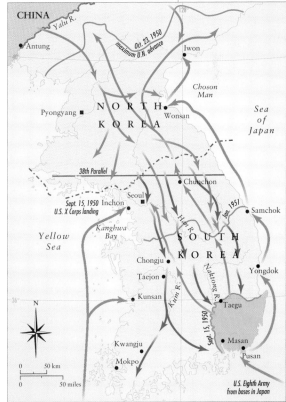

141

VIETNAM, 1961–1973

INDOCHINA WAR

☐ French Indochina

▨ Vietminh control, 1946–50

• French garrison north of 16th parallel after "free state" agreements, March 1946

▨ Vietminh control, 1950–54

→ French expeditionary corps movement, October 1945–January 1946

➤ French expeditionary corps movement, March–July 1946

✕ major battle

The Vietnam War developed as a postscript to the conflict between the French, the former colonial rulers of Indochina before the Second World War, and the Communist-led Vietminh, organized by Ho Chi Minh and his brilliant general Vo Nyguyen Giap. In 1945, Ho Chi Minh proclaimed the establishment of the Democratic Republic of Vietnam in Hanoi. Britain occupied Saigon in the south using Japanese troops, and then transferred power back to the French colonial authorities when French troops arrived. France recognized the new state but could not reach satisfactory economic and political agreements. Hostilities broke out between the Vietminh and the French, who backed the former emperor, Bao Dai. The Vietminh fought ferociously, and a last resort by the French was to occupy and fortify the town of Dien Bien Phu in an attempt to cut Ho's supply lines. Giap surrounded the French, pounded them with artillery, and overran the base in May 1954. A French collapse of will led to the partition of Indochina along the 17th parallel, with the North becoming Communist and the South ruled from Saigon, where Bao Dai was ousted in 1955 by Diem, who proclaimed a republic in October. His dictatorship, confused and badly run, attacked Buddhists and refused any referendum on reunification. Communist sympathizers who had fled north after partition began drifting back and established the Vietcong, which mounted guerrilla attacks on Diem's government and bases housing U.S. military advisors sent by President Eisenhower in 1954. The intensification of the attacks led the United States to bolster South Vietnam with a treaty of friendship and cooperation (April 1961). In December 1961, the first U.S. troops arrived, and by 1962, over 11,000 U.S. soldiers were stationed in Vietnam. In 1963, a military coup removed Diem over his failure to defeat the Communists or curb Buddhist unrest. Following a North Vietnamese attack on the U.S. destroyer *Maddox* in international waters in the Gulf of Tonking, the U.S. Congress authorized the president to "take all necessary measures to repel any armed

South Vietnamese government troops at a street checkpoint near the end of the Vietnam War.

attacks against forces of the United States." This famous resolution led to an escalation in warfare, with an air bombardment of North Vietnam followed by President Johnson's announcing an increase in U.S. forces in Vietnam to 125,000. By 1967, U.S. troops in South Vietnam numbered 463,000, supported by air force units and warships. In spite of this show of force, the Vietcong and North Vietnamese launched the Great Tet offensive in some thirty South Vietnamese cities. Although the campaign failed, the U.S. and world opinion were impressed by Vietcong strategy and endurance. Early in Nixon's presidency, he outlined peace proposals involving the withdrawal of all foreign forces from South Vietnam (U.S. troops had been joined by New Zealand and Australian forces under SEATO auspices) and a new policy of Vietnamization, that is, letting the Vietnamese deal with their own problems. By 1973, U.S. withdrawal was complete, but the battle-hardened North Vietnamese army moved south and invaded from border areas in Laos and Cambodia, destroying all resistance, capturing Saigon in 1975, and finally unifying a burned and battered Vietnam.

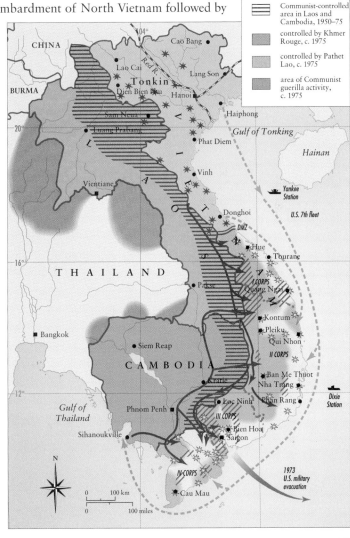

SOUTH ASIA: CONFLICT AND GROWTH

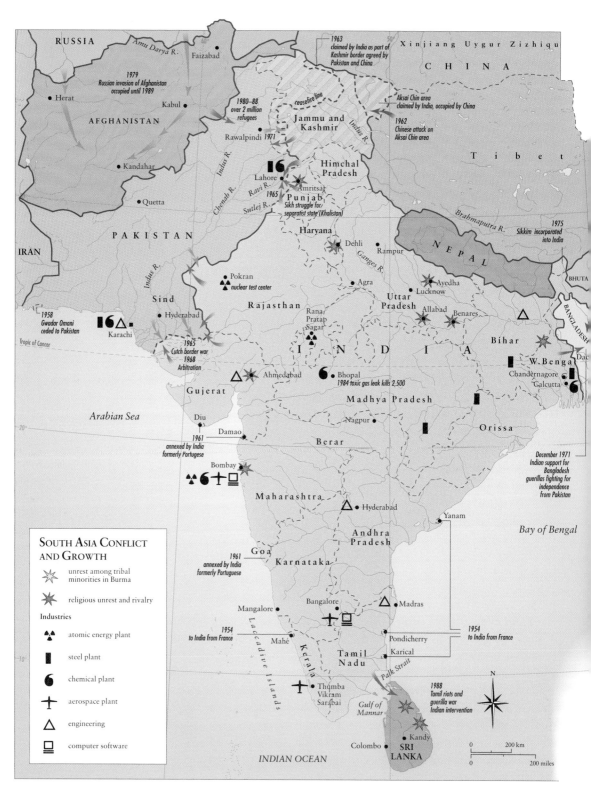

RUSSIA

Amu Darya R.

• Faizabad

1979
Russian invasion of Afghanistan
occupied until 1989

• Herat

Kabul •

AFGHANISTAN

1980–88
over 2 million
refugees

ceasefire line

Rawalpindi 1971

1963
claimed by India as part of
Kashmir border agreed by
Pakistan and China

X i n j i a n g   U y g u r   Z i z h i q u

C H I N A

Jammu and
Kashmir

Indus R.

Aksai Chin area
claimed by India, occupied by China

1962
Chinese attack on
Aksai Chin area

T i b e t

• Kandahar

Indus R.

Chenab R.

Lahore
Ravi R.

Amritsar

1965

Himchal
Pradesh

Punjab
Sikh struggle for
separatist state (Khalistan)

• Quetta

PAKISTAN

Sutlej R.

Haryana

Dehli

• Rampur

Ganges R.

N E P A L

Brahmaputra R.

1975
Sikkim incorporated
into India

IRAN

Indus R.

• Pokran
nuclear test center

• Agra

Ayedha
• Lucknow

BHUTA

1958
Gwadar Omani
ceded to Pakistan

Sind

• Hyderabad

Rajasthan

Rana
Pratap
Sagar

Uttar
Pradesh

Allabad

Benares

BANGLADESH

Tropic of Cancer

Karachi

1965
Cutch border war
1968
Arbitration

I N D I A

Bihar

W. Bengal

Dac

Chandernagore
Calcutta

Ahmedabad

• Bhopal
1984 toxic gas leak kills 2,500

Gujerat

Madhya Pradesh

Arabian Sea

Diu

• Nagpur

Orissa

Damao

1961
annexed by India
formerly Portuguese

Berar

Bombay

December 1971
Indian support for
Bangladesh
guerillas fighting for
independence
from Pakistan

Maharashtra

• Hyderabad

Yanam

Bay of Bengal

SOUTH ASIA CONFLICT AND GROWTH

Andhra
Pradesh

Goa

1961
annexed by India
formerly Portuguese

Karnataka

Madras

unrest among tribal
minorities in Burma

religious unrest and rivalry

Industries

Bangalore

1954
to India from France

Lacadive Islands

Mangalore •

Mahé

Pondicherry

Karical

1954
to India from France

atomic energy plant

steel plant

chemical plant

aerospace plant

engineering

computer software

Tamil
Nadu

Palk Strait

Thumba
Vikram
Sarabai

*Gulf of
Mannar*

1988
Tamil riots and
guerilla war
Indian intervention

N

Colombo •

• Kandy

SRI
LANKA

0   200 km

0   200 miles

INDIAN OCEAN

Since independence in 1947, India and Pakistan have sought to develop economically. The former has outstripped the latter in every sense, acquiring an industrial base that places India in the top twenty nations. Despite its large supply of educated people, transport, and a communications network, India retains the basic economic problem of supplying the needs of an expanding population. Foreign aid culled from both the United States and the USSR during Nehru's exploitation of nonalignment helped the early stages of economic growth. Some industrial plants have proved unsatisfactory, evidenced by the Union Carbide Corporation's factory at Bhopal which, in 1984, leaked toxic gas, killing some 2,500 people. The large-scale oil and nuclear energy plants and export industries require huge investments to eradicate economic hardship, conflict in the caste system, and linguistic divisions.

Sikh separatists' terror campaigns ensured military action by the government against the fortified Golden Temple of Amritsar. Mutinies by Sikh soldiers followed, and Prime Minister Indira Ghandi was murdered by her Sikh bodyguards. Hindu-Muslim violence occurred in 1990 at Ayedha, and high-low Hindu caste conflict was generated by positive job discrimination in favor of low castes.

India's nonaligned foreign policy was adequate regarding the Cold War but failed to protect her in regional disputes with Pakistan and China. On independence, Pakistani tribesmen helped the Muslim population of Kashmir to rebel against its Hindu ruler, who was supported by Indian troops. A United Nations–sponsored cease-fire in 1949 left Kashmir split in two. In 1965, moves to integrate the Indian-controlled areas into India itself occasioned conflict, which spread from Kashmir to the disputed border areas in the Rann of Cutch and the Punjab. The border in Gujerat was successfully arbitrated by British prime minister Harold Wilson, but the Kashmir issue remains unsolved. The last major conflict between India and Pakistan occurred in 1971, when Indian forces were sent into East Pakistan to aid the Bengalis seeking autonomy from West Pakistan. The Indian army captured Pakistani forces, and East Pakistan became Bangladesh. Disputes with China took place in the Aksai Chin in Kashmir, where China built strategic roads, and in Arunachal Pradesh, where the Chinese advanced almost to the plains of Assam. The Chinese suddenly pulled back in Arunachal Pradesh but kept the Aksai Chin. Elsewhere, South Asia has seen conflict in Burma, Sri Lanka, and war-torn and factionalized Afghanistan. In Burma, ethnic minorities in the Shan, Karen, and Kachin areas have seen separatist movements attacked by government troops. The Burmese military dictatorship has faced prodemocracy demonstrations. After the National League for Democracy (founded in 1988) won overwhelmingly in the 1990 legislative elections, the military refused to relinquish power and placed the opposition leader, Daw Aung San Suu Kyi, under house arrest from 1989 to 1995. The Soviet invasion of Pakistan (1979–1989) in support of Kabul Communists failed dismally, leaving resistance movements fighting each other, with the Taliban seemingly successful in 1997. In Sri Lanka, Tamil demands for a separate state (Eelam) developed into insurgency in 1985, and civil war with the majority Sinhalese continues today.

THE ASIAN ECONOMIC MIRACLE

Certain Asian economies have achieved phenomenal growth rates since the 1950s. China and Japan are the major components in an interlocking economy that covers the Pacific Rim with the "tiger" economies of South Korea, Taiwan, Hong Kong, and Singapore. In turn, trade from Asia is linked to Australia, New Zealand, and the U.S. West Coast cities. The other area of Asian economic development is the Middle East where oil is cheap to extract, and this helped industrial countries to switch energy from coal to oil. During the 1960s, the Organization of Petroleum Exporting Countries (OPEC) was established. Its twelve members, including non-Asian Nigeria and Venezuela, meet to coordinate oil policies. OPEC was formed when oil prices were falling through overproduction. Some oil-producing countries

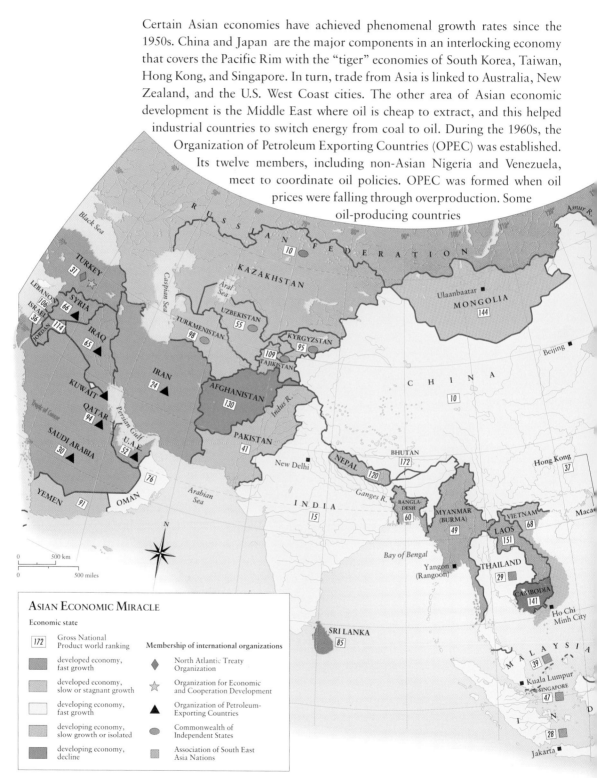

ASIAN ECONOMIC MIRACLE

Economic state

| 172 | Gross National Product world ranking |

developed economy, fast growth

developed economy, slow or stagnant growth

developing economy, fast growth

developing economy, slow growth or isolated

developing economy, decline

Membership of international organizations

◆ North Atlantic Treaty Organization

☆ Organization for Economic and Cooperation Development

▲ Organization of Petroleum-Exporting Countries

⬭ Commonwealth of Independent States

▢ Association of South East Asia Nations

have nationalized oil production and refining plants of oil companies and now enjoy huge incomes, which have been invested in developing a broader economic base or invested in the industrialized countries. During the 1973 Arab-Israeli War, Arab states cut oil sales to persuade the West to exert pressure on Israel. This failed, and since the 1990 Iraqi invasion of Kuwait, Arab cooperation has decreased, and so has OPEC's strength.

Japan was responsible for triggering Asian prosperity. The Japanese government planned economic development, concentrating its energies on domestic growth and export industries. High levels of technical education, labor discipline, and large industrial enterprises helped Japan to develop new technologies, especially in electronic equipment and computers. Many companies are multinationals and invest heavily abroad, building car factories, such as Toyota in Derbyshire, England. Japanese success spawned imitators in the four tiger economies that focused on export-led growth industries. Their outstanding results have generated sufficient profits that they are now investing in Malaysia, Thailand, Indonesia, and the Philippines, allowing these to commence their own economic expansion. Singapore is a prime example of a successful tiger economy. Ruled by the People's Action Party, an occasionally authoritarian organization, political stability has aided an economic boom. Providing a base for foreign multinationals, Singapore uses international banking and tourism as sources of revenue. The Jurong Industrial Estate has over 1,600 factories, and Singapore produces goods as diverse as chemicals, pharmaceuticals, electronics, steel pipes, plywood, bricks, and cement. Ship and oil-rig building are important industries, to be expected in one of the best Asian ports. Owing to its geographical position, Singapore is an important transshipment point, aided by one of the largest international airports in Asia. Taiwan is noted for its manufacture and export of electrical equipment, including radios, TVs, videos, and microcomputers. Hong Kong, similarly, had a limited democracy under British rule, and bases its wealth on foreign trade, manufacturing, and the reexport business. The future of Hong Kong is now uncertain since its return in 1997 to Chinese sovereignty. Overall, the Pacific Rim is the fastest growing economic development area in the world. Its profits invested in Europe and the United States are a historic irony, and the dependence of the tigers on Middle Eastern oil and gas is another.

MODERN CHINA

In the 1950s, the government turned its attention to the economy, by increasing agricultural production and introducing land reform that placed greater emphasis upon rural communities, while creating, at the same time, a heavy industrial base predicated upon central planning carried out by technocrats through the implementation of five-year plans that were not dissimilar to the Soviet model. However, in 1958, Mao Tse-tung (alternatively Mao Zedong), dissatisfied with the pace of change, introduced "The Great Leap Forward," basing the organization of production upon the egalitarianism and revolutionary zeal of rural communes and urban associations. The project failed, due to disastrous harvests and poor products that slowed down the rate of economic growth and created a serious rift between radicals and moderates within the Party. The Great Leap Forward came to a standstill and was abandoned in 1961.

Ever the ideologist, Mao intervened once again in 1965, supported by the Party radicals who

had fully backed the Great Leap Forward. This time Mao launched the "Great Proletarian Cultural Revolution" (1965–1969), introducing a "Permanent Revolution," led by students and young workers who organized themselves as the seven-million-strong Red Guard who attempted to wipe away what were perceived to be careerism, bureaucratic expertise, and bourgeois thinking within the Communist Party establishment. In a series of demonstrations and attacks upon individuals and property, chaos, violence, confusion, and misery ensued, as teachers, artists, intellectuals, and civil servants were harassed. The Cultural Revolution also produced a breakdown of the Chinese education system and a downturn in economic growth, in sharp contrast to the spectacular achievements of China's neighbors in the Far East.

Excluded from the United Nations and unrecognized by the United States, China strove to play a major role on the world stage. Having been fully committed to supporting North Korea during the Korean War—a hot point of the Cold War—China proceeded to play a key role in the Geneva Conference of 1954, which settled the war that had been fought between France and Vietnam since 1946. China also contributed significantly to the Bandung Conference of non-aligned countries in 1955. In the meantime, Sino-Soviet relations remained cordial throughout the 1950s, with Mao traveling to Moscow in 1957. The end of the decade witnessed a downturn in relations due to conflicting Party ideologies and disputes over border territories, most notable of which was the border clash in Siberia in 1969.

China began to realign with the West with the official visit to China of U.S. president Richard Nixon in 1972. Four years later, Mao died and was succeeded by the more pragmatic Deng Xiaoping. Deng introduced economic reforms, covering agriculture, industry, defense, and technology. Although these had first been introduced by Mao in 1963, they had been abandoned in favor of ideology during the Cultural Revolution. Deng reestablished material incentives with the "Responsibility System," whereby the power of management was transferred from the commune to the individual. He also encouraged the decentralization of economic management, foreign trade, and investment. Agricultural production was stimulated by giving individual farmers control over their land. Relations with both the West and the Soviet Union improved. The Cultural Revolution was denounced, and in 1976, the "Gang of Four," led by Mao's fourth wife, were arrested and put on trial, allegedly for plotting to seize power. In 1981, they were convicted of treason and were blamed for the excesses of the Cultural Revolution. Armed with a new party constitution he introduced in 1982, Deng made a complete break with the Maoist past.

Hand in hand with these developments came popular demands for increased political freedoms. These came to a head with the prodemocracy protests in Tienanmen Square, Beijing, in the spring and summer of 1989. Martial law was proclaimed on May 20, and the demonstrators were violently crushed by the state at the beginning of June, when thousands were massacred by units of the People's Liberation Army. This development was in clear contradistinction to the collapse of communism in eastern and central Europe, following a wave of prodemocracy protests.

Despite tremendous industrial growth in the cities and the coastal regions of China, the rural way of life remains largely unchanged.

CHRONOLOGY

9000 BC   Agriculture and animal husbandry. Earliest settlements in Near East.

8000 BC   Jericho, the earliest walled city.

6000 BC   Settlement of Catal-Hüyük in Anatolia; earliest pottery and textiles.

5000 BC   Irrigation around Tigris River (Mesopotamia).

3200 BC   City at Long-shan (China). Use of wheel and plow in Mesopotamia.

3000 BC   Cities in Mesopotamia.

2750 BC   Cities along Indus River.

2500 BC   Horse domesticated, Asian steppe region.

2330 BC   World's earliest empire established along the Euphrates by Sargon of Agade.

2000 BC   Hittites invade Anatolia; use of cuneiform script.

1750 BC   Rise of Babylon under Hammurabi.

1600 BC   Bronze-working cities in China.

1550 BC   Aryans invade Indus Valley and northern India. Emergence of Shang dynasty in China.

1400 BC   Assyrian Empire fouded.

1200 BC   Hittite empire in Near East collapses. Jews from Egypt settle in Palestine; foundation of Judaism.

1100 BC   Aryans spread along Ganges River.

1022 BC   Chou ousts Shang dynasty in China.

800 BC   Aryans spread into southern India. Earliest oral Upanishads.

771 BC   Chou dynasty ousted in China.

650 BC   Iron-working in China. Earliest coins in Lydia, Near East.

612 BC   Nineveh overrun by Scythians under Medes; collapse of Assyrian empire.

586 BC   Oppression of Jews in Babylon.

550 BC   The Persians under Cyrus II conquer the Scythians; foundation of Persian empire and spread of Zoroastrianism.

521 BC   Persian empire under Darius I at its height.

403-221 BC   "Feuding States" period in China. Development of Chinese law.

334 BC   Alexander the Great conquers Persian empire.

329 BC   Alexander reaches India.

321 BC   Mauryan empire established by Chandragupta (Magadha, India).

312 BC   Seleucid dynasty founded in Syria.

262 BC   Mauryan emperor Asoka becomes Buddhist.

247 BC   Parthian kingdom established by Arsaces I.

221 BC   Shih Huang-ti unites China (Ch'in dynasty).

202 BC   Beginning of Han dynasty in China; capital at Ch'ang-an.

141 BC   Han Wu-ti extends Chinese Han empire eastward.

130 BC   Mongolian Tocharians found kingdom in Transoxania.

112 BC   Silk Road extends from China through central Asia to Europe.

64 BC   Roman emperor Pompey the Great conquers Syria; Seleucid empire collapses.

53 BC   Romans defeated by Parthians at Battle of Carrhae.

AD 9   In China, Wang Mang overthrows Han dynasty.

AD 25   Han dynasty restored, capital at Lo-yang.

AD 30   Jesus of Nazareth crucified in Jerusalem.

AD 60   Growth of Kushan empire.

AD 70   Jewish temple in Jerusalem demolished by Romans.

AD 78   Kushan under Kanishka invade northern India.

AD 91   Chinese defeat Mongolian Hsiung-nu (Huns).

AD 150   Buddhism spreads to China.

AD 184   Yellow Turban rebellions in Han China.

AD 200   Formulation of Mishnah Jewish law.

AD 220   Han dynasty collapses; tripartite division of China.

AD 224   Sasanian dynasty established in Persia.

AD 304   Hsiung-nu (Huns) invade China.

AD 320   Chandragupta I establishes Gupta empire in northern India.

AD 350   Huns invade Persia and India.

AD 480   Gupta empire collapses.

531   In Persia, Khosroes I extends Sasanian empire.

c. 550   Buddhism spreads to Korea and Japan.

589   Sui dynasty reunifies China.

607   Tibet unified.

611   Persians capture Antioch and Jerusalem; control Near East.

617   Civil strife in China.

622   Mohammed's Hejira to Medina; spread of Islam.

624   Order restored in China by T'ang dynasty.

632   Beginning of Arab expansion.

636   Battle of Yarmuk River; Arabs invade Syria and Iraq.

646   Fujiwara's Taika Reforms in Japan. Buddhism spreads to Tibet.

658   T'ang Chinese control Afghanistan, Kashmir, Sogdiana, and Oxus Valley.

665   Tibetans expand to Tsinghai and Turkestan.

676   Korea unified.

712   Arab conquest of Sind and Samarkand.

718   Arab siege of Constantinople fails.

745   Rise of Mongolian Uighur empire.

750   Establishment of Abbasid Arab caliphate.

751   Battle of Talas River between Abbasids and T'ang Chinese.

755   Rebellion in China led by An Lu-shan.

794   Japanese move capital from Nara to Kyoto.

800   Kingdom of Angkor (Cambodia) established by Jayavarman II. Shailendra kings construct temple of Borobudur (Java).

836   War for control of Deccan (India).

840   Collapse of Uighur empire.

842   Collapse of Tibetan empire.

907   T'ang dynasty ends.

916   Establishment of Khitan kingdom in Mongolia.

918   Beginning of Koryo dynasty in Korea.

935   Authorized text of the Koran.

936   Baghdad caliphate collapses.

939   Vietnam gains independence from China.

947   Khitans invade China; Liao dynasty in Peking.

967   Fujiwara control Japan.

997   China reunited under Sung dynasty.

1018   Mahmud of Ghazni destroys Hindu city of Kanauj. Rajendra Chola invades Sri Lanka.

1021   Cholas invade Bengal.

1038   Formation of Hsi-hsia by Tanguts (northwest China).

1044   Rise of Pagan (Burma).

1055   Baghdad captured by Seljuk Turks.

1071   Byzantines defeated by Seljuks at Battle of Manzikert.

1096   Frankish crusaders invade Anatolia and Syria.

1126   China divided between northern Chin and southern Sung.

1150   Hindu temple built at Angkor Wat.

1170   Height of Srivijaya (Java) under Shailendra dynasty.

1175   Mohammed of Ghazni establishes Muslim rule in India; spread of Islamic architecture. Angkor empire flourishing in Cambodia.

1188   Crusader kingdoms crushed by Saladin.

1193   Zen Buddhism founded in Japan.

1206   Gengis Khan leads Mongol invasion of Asia. Sultanate founded in Delhi.

1220   Earliest kingdom in Thailand.

1234   Mongols overrun Chin empire; expand westward into Russia, Poland, Hungary, Bohemia, and the Near East.

1258   Mongols overcome Abbasid caliphate, destroy Baghdad.

1264   Kublai Khan establishes Mongol Yüan dynasty in China.

1279   Mongols invade southern China.

1299   Ottoman Turks invade Anatolia.

1349   Chinese expand through southeast Asia, found settlement in Singapore. Rise of Majaphit empire in Java.

1368   Foundation of Chinese Ming dynasty.

1370   Rise of Hindu Vijayanagar in southern India. Retreat of Mongol empire.

1380   Mongol emperor Tamerlane (Timur Link) embarks on short-lived campaigns of reconquest.

1392   Korea gains independence.

1394   Thais invade Cambodia; capital moved to Phnom Penh.

1402   Tamerlane defeats Ottomans at Battle of Ankara.

1405   Chinese start explorations of Indian Ocean.

1409 and 1410   Ming expeditions against the Mongols.

1424   Ming expedition against the Mongols.

1428   Chinese driven from Vietnam.

1471   Vietnamese expand southward to Champa.

1500   Safavid dynasty founded in Persia by Shah Ismail.

1511   Portuguese capture strategic port of Malacca (southern Malaysia).

1516-17 Ottomans conquer Syria, Arabia, and Egypt.

1526   Babur victorious at Battle of Panipat; conquers Delhi and founds Mughal (Muslim) dynasty.

1550   Mongols under Altan Khan invade northern China. Japanese begin raiding Chinese coast.

1557   Portuguese settlement established at Macao (China).

1565   Mughal empire extended to Deccan by Akbar.

1571   Spanish capture Philippine Islands.

1581   Russians under Yermak invade Siberia.

1598   Persian capital established at Isfahan by Shah Abbas I.

1609   Tokugawa shogunate in Japan.

1619   Dutch establish Batavia (Jakarta, Indonesia), founding East Indian empire.

1638   Russians reach Alaska and the Pacific.

1641   Dutch capture Malacca.

1644   Manchus found Ch'ing dynasty in China.

1649   Russians establish Okhotsk.

1674   Hindu Maratha kingdom under Sivaji.

1689   Russian-Chinese Treaty of Nerchinsk.

1696   Chinese invasion of northern Mongolia.

1707   Mughal empire declines.

1735   Wahabite regeneration of Islam begins.

1736   Safavids ousted by Nadir Shah.

1747   Ahmad Abdali establishes kingdom in Afghanistan.

1751   Chinese invade Tibet. French rule in Deccan and southeastern India.

1755   Burma reunited under Alaungpaya, capital at Rangoon.

1757   British defeat French at Battle of Plassey (Bengal).

1761   British capture Pondicherry. French ousted from India.

1793   Ottoman empire reformed by Selim III.

1796   British capture Sri Lanka.

1817   British found Hindu College (Calcutta); spread of British education in India.

1818   British overcome Marathas, establish Raj.

1819   Founding of British Singapore.

1824   British rule established in Burma and Assam.

1825   France claims Cochin China after persecution of Catholic converts.

1830   Russians invade Kazakhstan.

1839   British occupy Aden (Yemen).

1839-60   The Opium Wars.

1843   British rule established in Sind.

1849   British rule established in Punjab and Kashmir.

1850   Start of T'ai-p'ing revolt against Manchu rule in China.

1851   Thailand cedes Cambodia and Laos to France.

1854   U.S.-Japanese trade agreement.

1857   The Indian Mutiny.

1858   China opened to trade by Treaty of Tientsin.

1860   Russian-Chinese Treaty of Peking; Russians gain Ussuri. Koreans oppose European colonization.

1863-93   Cambodia, Cochin, Annam, Tonkin, and Laos become French protectorates.

1868   Meiji oust Tokugawa in Japan.

1879   British conquer Afghanistan.

1885   Indian National Congress founded.

1886   British capture northern Burma.

1887   Unification of French Indo-China.

1894-95   Sino-Japanese war.

1898   Hundred Days Reform in China.

1900   Boxer rebellion against foreigners suppressed in China.

1904   British divide Bengal. Russo-Japanese war; Japan gains Korea and Formosa (Taiwan).

1905   Revolt and unrest in Russian empire.

1906   Revolution in Persia. In India, Muslim

League founded to press for separate Islamic state.

1910   Japanese annex Korea.

1911   Manchus overthrown; Sun Yat-sen becomes first president of Chinese Republic.

1914-18   First World War; Turkey, ally of Germany, is defeated and partitioned. Japan sides with Allies, makes gains in Pacific and China.

1917   The Tsar abdicates; Bolshevik takeover in Russia. Balfour declaration promises Jewish homeland in Palestine. Sun Yat-sen's government fragments.

1919   Amritsar massacre; spread of Indian opposition to British rule. May 4th nationalist movement in China.

1920-25   Armenia, Azerbaijan, Georgia, Turkmenistan, Uzbekistan, Kyrgyzstan, Kazakhstan, and Tajikistan absorbed into communist Russian empire, the USSR.

1921   Chinese Communist Party (CCP) founded in Shanghai.

1923   Greeks expelled from Turkey. Progressive leader Atatürk overthrows last Ottoman Sultan, and founds secular republic.

1925   Reza Khan becomes reformist Shah of Persia. Chiang Kai-shek attempts reunification of China, attacks communists.

1931   Japanese invade Manchuria (Manzhouguo). Ho Chi Minh leads Indo-China Communist Party.

1932   Ibn Saud founds dynasty in Saudi Arabia.

1933   Japan invades Jehol.

1934   Mao Tse-tung (Mao Zedong) leads Long March of Chinese communists from south, becomes Chinese Communist Party leader.

1936   Japanese-German anti-communist pact.

1937   Japanese invade China.

1941   World War II. Japanese invade Thailand and French Indo-China. Japanese air-raid on U.S. fleet at Pearl Harbour. Japanese take Philippines and Hong Kong. Pro-German regime in Iraq toppled.

1942   Japanese invade Burma, occupy Dutch Indonesia and Papua New Guinea, take Singapore, raid Darwin, Australia. Americans bomb Tokyo. Japanese advance into China and through Burma towards India. Nationalist riots against British rule in India. Japanese-U.S. battles in Pacific.

1943   British/Indian forces resist Japanese in Burma. U.S. victories in Pacific.

1944   British/Indian victories at Imphal and Kohima. U.S. captures Philippines.

1945 US invasion of Okinawa. British/Indian forces recapture Rangoon. Japanese surrender in Hong Kong, Burma, Papua New Guinea, Singapore, and China. In Indonesia, Sukarno declares war for independence from Dutch. U.S. and Soviet armies partition Korea. Viet Minh capture Hanoi and Saigon; Ho Chi Minh becomes republican president.

1946 War in China between communists and Chiang Kai-shek's Kuomintang army. French attempt to reimpose rule in Indo-china resisted by Viet Minh; U.S. supports French.

1947 End of the British Raj in India; India and Pakistan (East and West) partitioned amidst sectarian massacres. Nehru becomes first Indian prime minister, Jinnah governor-general of Pakistan.

1948 State of Israel established; first Arab-Israeli war. Mahatma Gandhi assassinated. India-Pakistan war over Kashmir. Sri Lanka (Ceylon) gains independence from Britain; Sinhalese repression of Tamil minority begins.

1949 Communists under Mao Tse-tung victorious in China, proclaim People's Republic; Kuomintang exiled to Taiwan. Indonesia gains independence.

1950-53 The Korean War provoked by communist invasion of south; UN repels invasion to 38th parallel; country partitioned. Chinese invade Tibet. Chinese land reforms initiated.

1954 French defeated by Viet Minh at Dien Bien Phu. Laos, Cambodia, and South Vietnam gain independence. U.S. supports South Vietnamese against North Vietnamese communists under Ho Chi Minh.

1956 Second Arab-Israeli war.

1957 Communist government elected in Kerala, India. Malaysia (Malaya) gains independence from Britain; communist insurgency begins.

1959 Lee Kuan Yew elected in Singapore, steers colony to independence from Britain.

1960 Widespread famines in China after failure of Mao's Great Leap Forward. Chinese-Russian border disputes begin.

1961 U.S. takes combat role in Vietnamese war. Kuwait wins independence from Britain and is claimed by Iraq.

1962 Chinese-Indian border skirmishes. Coup and civil war in Aden; British ousted.

1963 Ba'athists seize power in Syria.

1965 Renewed India-Pakistan war over Kashmir. Military coup in Indonesia. Ferdinand Marcos elected president in Philippines. Thailand assists U.S. defense of South Vietnam.

1966 Maoist Cultural Revolution and purges in China. Military coup in Indonesia led by General Suharto.

1967 Third Arab-Israeli (Six Day) war. Israel seizes Sinai, Gaza strip, West Bank, and Golan Heights. UN proposes "land for security" solution. Ba'athists gain power in Iraq.

1970 Right-wing coup in Cambodia; King Sihanouk exiled, allies with communist Khmer Rouge.

1971 Civil war in East Pakistan; splits from West, becoming Bangladesh. Zulfikar Ali Bhutto wins election in (West) Pakistan.

1972 U.S. President Nixon visits China; liberalization of Chinese foreign policy begins. Martial law imposed in Philippines.

1973 Fourth Arab-Israeli war.

1974 Khmer Rouge seizes power in Cambodia; Pol Pot's infamous "killing fields" regime.

1975 Fall of Saigon; U.S. withdraws from Vietnam. Indonesia invades East Timor.

1976 Syria invades Lebanon, ends civil war. Deng Xiao-ping starts modernization of China.

1977 Military coup in Pakistan led by Zia ul-Haq.

1978 Camp David peace treaty between Egypt and Israel. Vietnamese invade Cambodia; Pol Pot flees.

1979 Shah of Iran toppled by Ayatollah Khomeini. Russians invade Afghanistan. Saddam Hussein seizes power in Iraq. Bhutto executed in Pakistan. Persecution of Chinese in Vietnam leads to Nine-day war.

1980 Start of Iran-Iraq war. Military government in Turkey.

1982 Israel invades Lebanon, withdraws from Sinai. Civil war starts between Sinhalese and Tamils in Sri Lanka.

1984 Amritsar Golden temple occupied by Sikh separatists; stormed by Indian troops.

1987 Indian troops sent to Sri Lanka to subdue Tamil separatists. Corazon Aquino wins election in Philippines; Marcos indicted. Economic boom underway in South Korea.

1988 Iran-Iraq war ends. Iraqi chemical attacks on Kurds. Palestinian intifada rebellion in Israel. Benazir Bhutto elected in Pakistan. Widespread civil unrest in Burma (Myanmar), leading to military coup. Muslim fundamentalist riots in Mecca, Saudi Arabia.

1989 Russians withdraw from Afghanistan; factional civil war ensues. Student demonstrations for democratic reform in China end in Tienanmen Square massacre. Vietnamese withdraw from Cambodia; resurgence of

Khmer Rouge, UN intervention. In India, right-wing Hindu party leads coalition government. Stockmarket collapse in Japan.

1990 Iraq's Saddam Hussein invades Kuwait and threatens Saudi Arabian oilfields. Arab coalition backs U.S.-led Desert Storm to recapture Kuwait. Iraq driven back; UN sanctions and restrictions imposed. Armenian war in Azerbaijan over Nagorno-Karabakh enclave. Elections in Myanmar; Aung San Suu Kyi arrested. Indian troops withdrawn from Sri Lanka; Tamil rebellion continues.

1991 In Iraq, Shi'a and Kurdish rebellions crushed; exodus of Kurdish refugees. Armenia, Azerbaijan, Georgia, Turkmenistan, Uzbekistan, Kyrgyzstan, and Tajikistan declare independence from USSR; Kazakhstan granted autonomy.

1992 In India, Hindu extremists destroy mosque in Ayodhya; sectarian violence spreads. U.S. abandons bases in the Philippines. Introduction of market economy in China sparks rapid industrial growth, especially in south. Pacific rim trade boom; rising Asian nations branded "tiger economies."

1993 Riots in Bombay; stock exchange bombed. North Korea refuses to sign nuclear non-proliferation treaty.

1997 Handover of Hong Kong from British to Chinese. Stockmarket and bank collapses and financial scandals in Japan, Thailand, Malaysia, South Korea and Indonesia threaten the tiger economies boom.

1998 India tests atomic bomb followed by Pakistan three weeks later.

SELECT BIBLIOGRAPHY

The authors readily acknowledge the work of many scholars and publications that have been consulted in the preparation of this atlas. Following is a selected bibliography of works recommended for further reading on the topics covered in this atlas.

Ahsan, Aitzaz, *The Indus Saga and the Making of Pakistan,* Oxford University Press, 1997

Allchin, B. and R., *The Birth of Indian Civilization,* London, 1968

Barnshart, Michael A., *Japan and the World since 1868,* Arnold, 1995

Beasley, W. G., *Japanese Imperialism,* Oxford University Press, 1991

Begley, Vimala, and De Puma, Richard Daniel (eds), *Rome and India: The Ancient Sea Trade,* University of Wisconsin Press, 1992

Berger, Mark T. and Borer, Douglas A. (eds), *The Rise of East Asia, Critical Visions of the Pacific Century* Routledge, 1997

Brown, T. Louise, *War and Aftermath in Vietnam,* Routledge, 1991

Cain, P. J. and Hopkins, A. G., *British Imperialism, Crisis and Deconstruction 1914-1990,* Longman, 1993

Cain, P. J. and Hopkins, A. G., *British Imperialism, Innovation and Expansion 1688-1914,* Longman, 1993

Cambridge Encyclopaedia of China, Cambridge University Press, 1991

Ch'en, K. K. F., *Buddhism in China, a Historical Survey,* Princeton U. P., 1972

Clarke, J. J., *Oriental Enlightenment,* Routledge, 1997

Cook, M. A. (Ed), *A History of the Ottoman Empire to 1730,* New Haven, 1986

Cortazzi, H., *The Japanese Achievement,* St. Martin's Press, 1990

Costello, John, *The Pacific War,* William Collins and Son Ltd., 1981

Cotterell, A., *The Penguin Encyclopedia of Ancient Civilizations,* Penguin, 1988

Crossley, Pamela Kyle, *The Manchus,* Blackwell, 1996

Daniel, Glyn, *The First Civilizations, The Archaeology of their Origins,* Thames and Hudson, 1968

De Schweintz, Karl, *The Rise and Fall of British India: Imperialism as Inequality,* Routledge, 1983

Dryer, E. L., *China at War, 1901-1949,* Longman, 1995

Eberhard, W., *A History of China,* Routledge and Kegan Paul, 1950

Fisher, Michael H., *The Politics of the British Annexation of India, 1757-1857,* Oxford University Press, 1997

Fitzgerald, C. P., *China, A Short Cultural History,* Cresset Press, London, 1961

Flowerdew, John, *The Final Years of British Hong Kong,* Macmillan, 1997

Garnaut, R. and Drysdale, P. (eds), *Asia Pacific Regionalism, Readings in International Economic Relations,* Harper Educational, 1994

Godement, François, *The New Asian Renaissance, From Colonialism to the Post-Cold War,* Routledge, 1996

Graff, E. and Hammond, H. E., *South-East Asia: History, Culture, People,* Cambridge, 1980

Gray, Jack, *Rebellions and Revolutions, China from the 1800s to the 1980s,* Oxford University Press, 1990

Graz, Liesl, *The Turbulent Gulf, People, Politics and Power,* I. B. Turis, 1992

Gupta, Ashin Das, *Merchants of Maritime India,* Ashgate, 1994

Hall, D. G. E., *A History of South East Asia,* Macmillan, 1968

Harris, David R., (ed), *The Origins and Spread of Agriculture and Pastoralism in Eurasia,* UCL Press, 1995

Hastings, Max, *The Korean War,* Macmillan, 1987

Hawks, J., *The First Great Civilizations: Life in Mesopotamia, the Indus Valley and Egypt,* Penguin, 1977

Hintze, Andrea, *The Mughal Empire and its Decline,* Ashgate, 1997

Hucker, C., *China's Imperial Past,* Duckworth, 1975

Iriye, Akira, *The Origins of the Second World War in Asia and the Pacific,* Addison Wesley Longman, 1987

Jaffrelot, Christoffe, *The Hindu Nationalist Movement and Indian Politics, 1925 to the 1990s,* Columbia University Press, 1996

Jansen, Michael, Mulloy, Maire and Urban, Günter, *Forgotten Cities on the Indus, Early Civilization in Pakistan from the 8th to the 2nd Millennium BC,* Oxford University Press, 1996

Kramer, S. N., *History begins at Suma,* Thames and Hudson, 1961

Kramer, S. N., *Sumerian Mythology,* London and New York, 1963

Kristof, Nicholas D. and Wudunn, Sheryl, *China Wakes,* Nicholas Brealey Publishing, 1994

Kuhrt, Amelie, *The Ancient Near East c 3000-330 bc,* Routledge, 1997

Kunt, Martin (ed), *Suleyman the Magnificent and his Age,* Addison Wesley Longman, 1995

Lattimore, O., *The Steppes of Mongolia, and the Characteristics of Steppe Nomadism*, Bobbs-Merrill, 1975

Lattimore, O., *Inner Asian Frontiers of China*, New York, 1951

Le Heron, R, and Park, S. O., *The Asian Pacific Rim and Globalization*, Aldershot, 1995

Lengyell, Emil, *Asoka the Great: India's Royal Missionary*, Watts, 1969

Liu, Xinru, *Ancient India and Ancient China. Trade and Religious Exchanges, AD 1-600*, Oxford University Press, 1995

Lowe, Peter, *The Origins of the Korean War*, Addison Wesley Longman, 1997

Mabbett, I. W. and Chandler, David P., *The Khmers*, Blackwell, 1996

Macfie, A. L., *Atatürk*, Addison Wesley Longman, 1994

Maisels, Charles Keith, *Early Civilizations of the Old World, The Formative Histories of Egypt, the Levant, Mesopotamia, India and China*, Routledge, 1997

Maisels, Charles Keith, *The Emergence of Civilization, from Hunting and Gathering to Agriculture Cities and the State of the Near East*, Routledge, 1993

Mallory, J. P., *In Search of the Indo-European Language, Archaeology and Myth*, Thames and Hudson, 1991

Medley, M., *The Chinese Potter: A Practical History of Chinese Ceramics*, Phaidon, 1976

Megarry, Tim, *The Making of Modern Japan*, Greenwich University Press, 1995

Mellaart, J., *Early Civilizations of the Near East*, Thames and Hudson, 1975

Musallam, Ali, *The Iraqi Invasion of Kuwait, Saddam Hussein, His State and International Power Politics*, I. B. Tauris, 1995

Nizami, K. A., *South Asia*, Macmillan, 1997

O'Flaherty, W. D., *Hindu Myths*, Penguin, 1965

Ostrogorsky, G., *History of the Byzantine State*, Oxford, 1969

Ovendale, Ritchie, *The Origins of the Arab-Israeli Wars*, Addison Wesley Longman, 1992

Parry, V. J., *A History of the Ottoman Empire to 1730*, Cambridge Union Press, 1976

Pitcher, D. E., *An Historical Geography of the Ottoman Empire*, Leiden, 1973

Pitcher, A. H., *European Imperialism*, Macmillan, 1994

Porter, A. H., *European Imperialism*, Macmillan, 1994

Postgate, Nicholas, *Early Mesopotamia, Society and Economy at the Dawn of History*, Routledge, 1994

Postgate, J. N., *The First Empires*, Oxford, 1979

Raychaudhuri, H., *Political History of Ancient India. From the Accession of Parikhit to the Extinction of the Gupta Dynasty*, Oxford University Press, 1997

Robinson, Maxime, *Muhammed*, Penguin

Rodzinski, W., *The Walled Kingdom*, Fontana, 1991

Rohwer, Jim, *Asia Rising*, Nicholas Brealey Publishing, 1995

Rooney, Dawn, *Angkor, An Introduction to the Temples*, Odyssey, 1994

Runciman, Steven, *A History of the Crusades*, Cambridge University Press, 1951-54, 3 vols.

Sardesai, D. R., *South East Asia: Past and Present*, Macmillan, 1997

Shaw, Stanford J., *History of the Ottoman Empire and Modern Turkey, Vol I*, Cambridge University Press, 1976

Simkin, C. F., *The Traditional Trade of Asia*, Oxford, 1968

Stewart Macpherson, Joseph and Chang, Y.S. (eds), *Economic and Social Development in South China*, Edward TElgar Publishing Ltd., 1996

Stoneman, Richard, *Alexander the Great*, Routledge, 1997

Thapar, Romila, *Asoka and the Decline of the Mauryas*, Oxford University Press, 1997

Tully, Mark and Masari, Zareer, *From Raj to Rajiv*, BBC Books, 1988

Vernadsky, G. A., *The Mongols and Russia*, Yale University Press, 1953

Wheeler, Mortimer, *Indus Civilization*, Cambridge University Press, 1968

Yapp, M. E. *The Near East since the First World War*, Longman, 1991

Yung, Peter Xinjiang, *The Silk Road, Islam's Overland Route to China*, Oxford University Press, 1987

INDEX

ACKNOWLEDGMENTS

Pictures are reproduced by permission of, or have been provided by the following:

British Museum: pp. 20, 30.
Bibliothéque National, Paris, p. 84.
e.t. archive: pp. 25, 51, 63, 67, 72, 75, 88, 89, 91, 92, 95, 101, 102, 103, 111, 117, 119, 128.
Hulton Getty: pp. 94, 104, 113, 124, 126.
Robert Harding Picture Library, p. 24.
The Image Bank: pp. 36, 38, 44, 50, 60, 62, 106, 137, 149.
Peter Newark's Historical Pictures: pp. 29, 32.
Josephine Powell, Rome, p. 53.
National Museum, New Delhi, p. 63.
Victoria and Albert Museum, London, p. 64.
and Private Sources, p. 80.

Illustrations: Peter A. B. Smith and M. A. Swanston.

Design: Malcolm Swanston.

Typesetting: Shirley Ellis.

Cartography: Peter Gamble, Elsa Gibert, Peter A. B. Smith, Malcolm Swanston, Isabelle Verpaux, Jonathan Young.

Production: Marion M. Storz.